# Native Americans of the Northeast

# Native Americans of the Northeast

Stuart A. Kallen

Lucent Books, Inc.
P.O. Box 289011, San Diego, California

## Titles in the Indigenous Peoples of North America Series Include:

The Apache
The Cherokee
The Iroquois
Native Americans of the Great Lakes
Native Americans of the Northeast
Native Americans of the Plains
Native Americans of the Southeast
Native Americans of the Southwest
The Navajo
The Sioux

Library of Congress Cataloging-in-Publication Data

Kallen, Stuart A., 1955-
    Native Americans of the Northeast / by Stuart A. Kallen.
        p.    cm. — (Indigenous peoples of North America)
    Includes bibliographical references (p. ) and index.
    Summary: Discusses the history, daily lives, culture, religion, and
conflicts of the Indians that lived in the northeastern part of what is now the
United States, including the Algonquian, Abenaki, and Wampanoag tribes.
    ISBN 1-56006-629-6 (lib. : alk. paper)
    1. Indians of North America—New England—Juvenile literature.
2. Woodland Indians —Juvenile literature. [1. Indians of North America—
New England. 2. Woodland Indians.]  I. Title. II. Series.
    E78.N5K35   2000
    974'.00497—dc21                                    99-043151
                                                            CIP

Copyright 2000 by Lucent Books, Inc.
P.O. Box 289011, San Diego, California 92198-9011

Printed in the U.S.A.

# Contents

# Foreword

North America's native peoples are often relegated to history—viewed primarily as remnants of another era—or cast in the stereotypical images long found in popular entertainment and even literature. Efforts to characterize Native Americans typically result in idealized portrayals of spiritualists communing with nature or bigoted descriptions of savages incapable of living in civilized society. Lost in these unfortunate images is the rich variety of customs, beliefs, and values that comprised—and still comprise—many of North America's native populations.

The *Indigenous Peoples of North America* series strives to present a complex, realistic picture of the many and varied Native American cultures. Each book in the series offers historical perspectives as well as a view of contemporary life of individual tribes and tribes that share a common region. The series examines traditional family life, spirituality, interaction with other native and non-native peoples, warfare, and the ways the environment shaped the lives and cultures of North America's indigenous populations. Each book ends with a discussion of life today for the Native Americans of a given region or tribe.

In any discussion of the Native American experience, there are bound to be sim-

ilarities. All tribes share a past filled with unceasing white expansion and resistance that led to more than four hundred years of conflict. One U.S. administration after another pursued this goal and fought Indians who attempted to defend their homelands and ways of life. Although no war was ever formally declared, the U.S. policy of conquest precluded any chance of white and Native American peoples living together peacefully. Between 1780 and 1890, Americans killed hundreds of thousands of Indians and wiped out whole tribes.

The Indians lost the fight for their land and ways of life, though not for lack of bravery, skill, or a sense of purpose. They simply could not contend with the overwhelming numbers of whites arriving from Europe or the superior weapons they brought with them. Lack of unity also contributed to the defeat of the Native Americans. For most, tribal identity was more important than racial identity. This loyalty left the Indians at a distinct disadvantage. Whites had a strong racial identity and they fought alongside each other even when there was disagreement because they shared a racial destiny.

Although all Native Americans share this tragic history they have many distinct differences. For example, some tribes and individuals sought to cooperate almost immediately with the U.S. government while others steadfastly resisted the white presence. Life before the arrival of white settlers also varied. The nomads of the Plains developed altogether different lifestyles and customs from the fishermen of the Northwest coast.

Contemporary life is no different in this regard. Many Native Americans—forced onto reservations by the American government—struggle with poverty, poor health, and inferior schooling. But others have regained a sense of pride in themselves and their heritage, enabling them to search out new routes to self-sufficiency and prosperity.

The *Indigenous Peoples of North America* series attempts to capture the differences as well as similarities that make up the experiences of North America's native populations—both past and present. Fully documented primary and secondary source quotations enliven the text. Sidebars highlight events, personalities, and traditions. Bibliographies provide readers with ideas for further research. In all, each book in this dynamic series provides students with a wealth of information as well as launching points for further research.

# The First Americans

The northeastern region of the United States contains some of the oldest cities and towns in North America. Some population centers in the area such as New York and Boston are among the largest and wealthiest cities in the world. This region is also one of the most industrialized areas of the world, where tens of millions of people live, work, and play. Freeways, factories, office buildings, strip malls, and suburbs fill most of the landscape.

The first Europeans to arrive in the Northeast were fishermen in the early sixteenth century. By 1650, the northeastern region was known as New England and over fifty thousand migrants from Europe lived in the area. By 1750, over 1 million people originally from Great Britain, France, the Netherlands, Germany, and elsewhere had cut down forests, plowed the land, opened businesses, and built thousands of municipalities across the region. They were aided in this task by thousands of African American slaves. Today, the great majority of people in the region are descendants of immigrants from Europe, Africa, Latin America, and Asia.

But the land called New England wasn't new at all. It was the ancient homeland for almost one hundred thousand indigenous people named Indians by the whites and often referred to as "savages" and "heathens." As Tall Oak, a member of the Narragansett tribe states:

> When the Europeans first arrived [in the Caribbean,] Columbus and his crew, he came and he called us Indians, because of the obvious reason, he thought he was lost in India. But what did we call ourselves before Columbus came? That's the question so often asked. And the thing is in every single tribe, even today, when you translate the word that each had for ourselves, without knowledge of each other, it was always something that translated to basically the same thing. In our language it's *Ninuog*, or the people, the human beings. That's

what we called ourselves. So when the Pilgrims arrived here, we knew who we were, but we didn't know who they were. So we called them *Awaugangeesuck*, or the strangers, because they were the ones who were alien, they were the ones that we didn't know, but we knew each other. And we were the human beings.[1]

Until that time— and for more than ten thousand years—at least forty different tribes inhabited the modern-day states of Maine, New Hampshire, New York, New Jersey, Massachusetts, Connecticut, and Rhode Island. These natives also lived in the Canadian provinces of Nova Scotia, New Brunswick, and Quebec.

By the time the Europeans arrived, the Native Americans of the Northeast had highly developed and distinct cultures,

deeply spiritual religions based on nature, and intricately woven political alliances. They made everything they owned from natural materials, including their clothing, their canoes, and their shelters. The natives did not have horses, guns, or the wheel, but they did exhibit a mastery of hunting, fishing, and other skills needed to thrive in the American woodlands. These people were farmers, hunters, politicians, warriors, artisans, healers, and more.

As Native American historian Francis Jennings points out in *The Invasion of America,*

European explorers and invaders discovered an inhabited land. Had it been pristine wilderness then, it would possibly be so today, for neither the technology nor the social organization of Europe in the sixteenth

*Even in 1746, New York was a thriving urban area.*

9

and seventeenth centuries had the capacity to maintain, of its own resources, outpost colonies thousands of miles from home. Incapable of conquering true wilderness, the Europeans were highly competent in the skill of conquering other people, and that is what they did. They did not settle a virgin land. They invaded and displaced a resident population.[2]

## Deadly Clash of Cultures

The first Europeans to have contact with the northeast tribes were Italian, Spanish, English, and French explorers. The first written records of contact were made in 1524 when Giovanni da Verrazano anchored briefly off the coast of modern-day Manhattan. In 1609 Henry Hudson, an Englishman in the service of the Dutch East India Company, sailed up the Muhheakantuck, known today as the Hudson River. Later explorers brought trade goods to the natives such as guns, iron, the wheel, and other manufactured products. They also brought such deadly diseases as smallpox, measles, and cholera, against which Native Americans had little resistance.

In the early 1600s, thousands of Native Americans were killed by these European diseases. Author David Horowitz explains the details in *The First Frontier:*

In the winter of 1616 an infection ravaged the natives of the coastal territory known as New England. . . . An unprecedented force in the wilderness region, the plague [now believed to be smallpox] was brought by European traders and adventurers, whose ships touched land with increasing frequency, as the advance of a maritime empire.

In the two years during which the fever spread through their villages, perhaps a third of the peoples living between Narragansett Bay and the Piscataqua River died. Tribes that had been flourishing and strong grew weak; weak tribes disappeared.[3]

Conditions did not much improve for the native tribes of the Northeast after the initial diseases had run their course. In New Hampshire, for instance, a smallpox epidemic began along the Merrimack River in 1631 and lasted until 1635. Smallpox returned in 1639, followed by influenza in 1647, smallpox again in 1649, and diphtheria in 1659. These diseases in this one region reduced the Pennacook tribe from twelve thousand members to twelve hundred survivors within thirty years.

It was not only disease that affected the natives of the Northeast. The Pilgrims arrived from England in 1620, and within twenty years the Native Americans in the region were overwhelmed by the sheer number of settlers hungry for land, timber, minerals, fish, furs, and other riches. By the beginning of the nineteenth century, a great majority of the New England tribes were either extinct, reduced to small numbers, or had been forced to live elsewhere. A small percentage of the first Americans remained, living on small reservations or in villages and cities.

## Recording Native American History

Although hundreds of thousands of indigenous people lived in North America, Europeans believed they had "discovered" America, or, as it was called, the "New World." Cultural and religious conceit, however, kept the Europeans from appreciating the worthiness of the indigenous people and from recognizing the legiti-

macy of their claim to the land. Missionaries tried to force Native Americans to abandon their spiritual beliefs and convert to Christianity. French trappers used the natives to obtain pelts which were sold at great profit in Europe. English settlers simply forced the natives off the land, caring little where they went or what was to become of their ancient culture and knowledge.

Since the Native Americans did not have a written language until they adopted English (or French in Canada), most of what has been written about the tribes throughout the centuries was the work of

*Christopher Columbus landed in the West Indies in 1492, sparking European interest in the New World.*

outsiders, who often misunderstood or exaggerated aspects of Native American culture. In addition, many Native American religious beliefs and creation stories were distorted to fit in the concepts of God and the Devil as held by Christian believers. These biases have perpetuated many myths still seen in books, movies, and television shows.

The European view of Native Americans, while never flattering, depended on the time and place as well as the situation. As Francis Jennings writes in *The Invasion of America,* "When the Indians were regarded as partners in profitable trade, they appeared less threatening, and their [imagined] vices were

excused. When they resisted eviction from lands wanted by the colonizers, they acquired demonic dimensions."[4]

## Keeping the Tribal Flames Burning

Although the past three hundred years have not been kind to the Native American people, the United States is beginning to come to terms with the role its society has played in the near destruction of native culture. A small percentage, less than one-eighth, of northeast Native American tribes have become associated with gambling casinos in some highly visible areas, including the Foxwoods Casino in Led-

*The Foxwoods Casino in Connecticut is only one of several casinos run by Native American tribes.*

yard, Connecticut. For the first time in centuries, the tribes are amassing monetary and political capital. With this new-found wealth comes a renewal of pride.

Native Americans of the Northeast have greatly influenced the growth and prosperity of the United States and Canada since the first Europeans arrived in the 1600s.

They showed the first European colonists how to hunt, fish, grow food, and survive in an environment of which they had little understanding. In spite of the systematic attempts to destroy Native American culture, the first Americans have endured to preserve their heritage, tribal affinities, and distinctive religious beliefs.

# Chapter 1

# Native Peoples of the Northeast

Native Americans in the northeast region of the United States descended from ancient people called Paleo-Indians, who first moved to the area more than twelve thousand years ago, after the last glaciers of the Ice Age began their northward retreat. At that time, the climate was cold and harsh, and the Paleo-Indians hunted large herd animals such bison, mammoths, and mastodons with stone-tipped spears.

As the climate warmed, the huge mammals became extinct, but the gradual warming made it possible for the people to utilize a great diversity of evolving plant and animal species. This period, known as the Archaic period, lasted more than nine thousand years, from about 10,000 B.C. to around 700 B.C. During this time, Archaic people hunted smaller forest animals such as deer and rabbits and learned to survive on other food sources such as shellfish, herbs, berries, roots, nuts, and seeds. Hunters made more advanced stone implements such as axes,

knives, and other tools used for building wood shelters and dugout canoes.

The era that lasted from 700 B.C. to A.D. 1500 is known as the Woodland period. During this time, northeast Native Americans added farming to their hunting-and-gathering economy. The Woodland people farmed corn, beans, and squash to supplement their diets and also grew tobacco for ceremonial purposes. Pottery making was perfected and the stone bowls characteristic of the Archaic period were replaced with clay pottery.

With the addition of corn, beans, and squash to their diet, tribal populations were able to increase. As the size of the clans increased, more communities were built throughout the forests. Large communities called for more collective organization, giving rise to strong leaders and ruling families. A larger population also meant more competition for land and resources, and the later Woodland period was marked by tribal rivalries, warfare, and an elevated male warrior culture.

*During the Woodland period Native Americans incorporated farming into their culture, allowing for a consistent food supply.*

The warming climate also favored the northward migration of people with farming skills, who spread as far north as the Saco River in the present-day state of Maine near the New Hampshire border. Tribes who lived north of that boundary, however, continued with earlier patterns of hunting and gathering.

## The Ruling Sachems

Sachems were the main political leaders of the Woodland tribes. Each sachem (meaning "chief" or "leader") ruled over a small territorial domain called a sachemdom that was independent from other tribal sachemdoms in the area. On the island known today as Martha's Vineyard, for example, four sachems presided over four distinct regions, each one of which was divided into smaller subdivisions ruled by minor subsachems called sagamores.

The position of sachem was passed down along male hereditary lines from father to son or from elder brother to younger brother. In the absence of male heirs, the title could be passed to daughters or sisters, and several notable female sachems presided over northeastern tribes.

Sachems received guests, sponsored rituals, conducted diplomatic relations with other tribes, assigned hunting grounds, and administered justice. They were aided in these tasks by counselors and other assistants. Rather than rule by force, sachems generally relied on persuasion and tried to achieve consensus among the people. If the actions of a sachem were not acceptable to tribal members, his followers would defect to another sachem, who would more closely follow the will of the people.

Sachems collected tribute (what might be called taxes) from those who were granted rights to hunt or farm the land. This meant that sachems were given the skins of any deer killed in their ponds or rivers, the forequarters of any deer killed in their woods, and the first fruits and vegetables from the annual harvest. Sachems lived in larger shelters than other tribal members, enjoyed more wealth, and often married more than one wife. It was common, as well, for members of ruling families to intermarry, a practice that strengthened peaceful relations among independent groups.

## Tribes of the Dawnland

Powerful sachems were necessary because the vast northeastern region of the North American continent was populated by a large—and often confusing—number of tribes and subtribes who were constantly forging or breaking political alliances with one another.

## The Algonquian Language

All southern New England tribes spoke languages related to the Algonquian (sometimes spelled Algonkian, Algonkin, or Algonquin) language family. Different dialects of the language were spoken by tribes over a wide geographic area from New England to the northwestern shores of Lake Superior. It is estimated that the northeastern Woodland tribes spoke at least thirteen different languages, all related to the Algonquian family. Many words in modern usage come from the Algonquian language including hickory, moccasin, moose, papoose, powwow, squash, tomahawk, wigwam, and woodchuck.

In his book *The Delaware Indians,* Clinton Alfred Weslager explains the language classification.

"Although in most instances the dialects were mutually [understood] in extreme cases the difference between one Algonkian dialect and another was comparable to the difference between modern French and Spanish. . . . It came as a surprise to the early European explorers that, not only were different languages spoken by American Indian tribes, but some Indians could not understand others. . . .

The word *Algonkian* as applied to a family of Indian languages was derived from a small [tribe] that resided in Canada . . . known to the French as the Algonquin or Algonkin. The prominence of the tribe was not the result of it size, but of the emphasis given its customs and language in the writings of early French Jesuit missionaries. The Algonquin people were only [one] among many Indian groups who spoke the same language, and . . . their name became used arbitrarily as a generic for the language. . . . Hence, the word Algonkian, a modification of *Algonquin,* has come to apply to a family of related dialects."

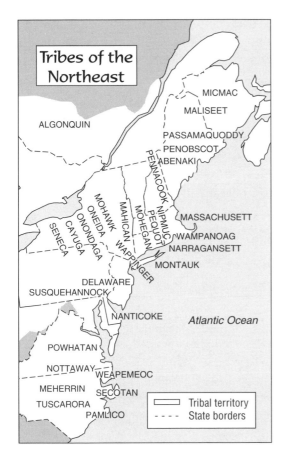

Tribes of the Northeast

MICMAC
MALISEET
ALGONQUIN
PASSAMAQUODDY
PENOBSCOT
ABENAKI
PENNACOOK
NIPMUC
MOHAWK
ONEIDA
ONONDAGA
CAYUGA
SENECA
MAHICAN
WAPPINGER
PEQUOT
MOHEGAN
MASSACHUSETT
WAMPANOAG
NARRAGANSETT
MONTAUK
DELAWARE
SUSQUEHANNOCK
NANTICOKE
POWHATAN
NOTTAWAY
WEAPEMEOC
MEHERRIN
SECOTAN
TUSCARORA
PAMLICO

Atlantic Ocean

☐ Tribal territory
- - - - State borders

The Abenaki were a good example. When Europeans arrived in New England, the tribe was a confederacy of Algonquian-speaking tribes who populated the present states of Maine, Vermont, New Hampshire, and elsewhere. The Abenaki were members of a larger group called the Wabanaki that included the Passamaquoddy and Maliseet tribes of eastern Maine and the Canadian province of New Brunswick. Today, as in the seventeenth century, the Abenaki are composed of two main branches, and the larger branch is divided into bands named after the rivers they set-

tled. These tribes include the Penobscot, Kennebec, Androscoggin, and Wawenock.

The western branch of the Abenaki lived to the south and west. According to *The Original Vermonters* by William A. Haviland and Marjory W. Power,

In Vermont, there were several major bands of western Abenakis, each of which was associated with a substantial village. These villages were located on canoeable streams near a major body of water: the Connecticut River on the east and Lake Champlain on the west. Historic sources mention an important Cowasuck village at Newbury . . . (*Kowasék,* or "Place of the White Pines"); and a Sokoki village at Northfield, Massachusetts, just south of Vermont. . . . In 1663, the Sokokis (from *Sohkwahkiak,* "The People Who Separated") established a new village at Fort Hill, north of the Ashuelot River. . . . In western Vermont, villages seem to have been located near the mouths of Otter Creek, the Winooski, Lamoille, and Missisquoi [Rivers]. Two of these survived late enough to be mentioned in historic sources: *Winoskik,* for which the Winooski River was named, and *Mazipskoik,* which was corrupted to Missisquoi.[5]

The Pennacook and Pawtucket tribes were aligned with the Abenaki and lived on the upper Merrimack River in New Hampshire, around present-day Concord.

Pennacook comes from the Abenaki word *penakuk,* meaning "at the bottom of the hill." The tribe, which lost most of its population as a result of devastating epidemics and war casualties, moved to Canada in the late seventeenth century and merged with the Sokoki to become the St. Francis Indians in Quebec.

The name Abenaki means "people of the Dawnland," or more simply "easterners," and refers to the rising sun which casts its first rays on Abenaki land. The Dawnland was a cold, snowy place with short summers, but it was also a region of azure lakes and sparkling rivers that spilled down through forested mountain ranges onto the rock-strewn beaches of the Atlantic Ocean. Streams from New Hampshire's White Mountains and Vermont's Green Mountains form the mighty Connecticut River, which

## Indian City Names

Both by accident and intent, European settlers decimated the tribes of Native Americans who populated the Northeast. However, many villages, towns, and cities in the region were named with Native American words. Native Americans even gave the New Englanders their nickname—the word "Yankee" is from a Native American pronunciation of "English" ("Yenguese").

Some of the places named after tribes were the state of Massachusetts and the cities of Niantic in Connecticut and Narragansett in Rhode Island and Montauk and Manhattan in New York. Words from the Delaware tribe were used to name Passaic and Hoboken, New Jersey, and Conestoga and Susquehanna, Pennsylvania. Words from the Abenaki tribe in Maine and Vermont were used to name the state of Connecticut ("long estuary"), and the cities of Kennebec ("long water without rapids") in

Maine, and Merrimac ("at the deep place") and Nashua ("between streams") in New Hampshire.

Other place names in New England:

Acadia—"the earth"

Androscoggin—"fish-curing place"

Appalachian—"people of the other side"

Chappaquiddick—"separated island"

Chicopee—"rushing water"

Cohasset—"young pine island"

Cuttyhunk—"thing that lies out in the sea"

Hoosac—"mountain rock"

Mystic—"great tidal river"

Ossipee—"rocky river"

Pawtuxet—"little falls"

Saco—"outflowing"

Saranac—"river of sumac trees"

Taconic—"wilderness"

Winnipesaukee—"lakeland"

Woonsocket—"a place of deep descent"

the Native Americans called *Kwini tekw,* "the long river." Tall mountain peaks such as Mount Washington scrape the clouds and were regarded by the Abenaki as sacred places where powerful spirits resided.

# The People of the East

South of the Dawnland in present-day Massachusetts, along the shores and wetlands of Massachusetts Bay, lived the Massachusett tribes. By the time the Puritan colonists began streaming into Massachusetts Bay in the 1640s, however, these tribes were virtually extinct—victims of an epidemic brought by European seamen. An Englishman named Thomas Morton, who lived among the Massachusetts, wrote about the epidemic which raged for several years beginning in 1617:

> The hand of God fell heavily upon them with such a mortall stroake that they died on heapes, as they lay in their houses. . . . For in a place where many inhabited, there hath been but one a live, to tell what became of the rest, the livinge being (as it seemes) not able to bury the dead. . . . And the bones and skulls upon severall places of their habitations, made such a spectacle after my comming into those partes, that as I travailed in the Forrest, nere the Massachussets, it seemed to mee a new found Golgotha [place of the skull].[6]

The Wampanoag ("People of the East," or "People of the Dawn"), also known as the Pokanokets ("Place of the Clear Land") lived in the region of today's Buzzards Bay. Before the Europeans, there were an estimated twenty-four thousand Wampanoags in southeastern Massachusetts and the eastern part of Rhode Island. Their lands contained deep forests of oak, pine, and maple divided by wetlands, rivers, and streams.

The Nauset tribe lived east of the Wampanoag territory, in Cape Cod, the long peninsula in southeastern Massachusetts. Sometimes referred to as the Cape Indians, the Nausets never numbered more than fifteen hundred before the epidemics. French sea captain Samuel de Champlain, one of the first Europeans to have contact with the Nausets, described their appearance in his journal, later published as *Voyages of Samuel de Champlain 1604–1618:*

> We saw in this place some five to six hundred savages, all naked except their sexual parts, which they cover with a small piece of doe or sealskin. The women are also naked, and, like the men, cover theirs with skins or leaves. They wear their hair carefully combed and twisted in various ways, both men and women. . . . Their bodies are well-proportioned, and their skin olive-colored. They adorn themselves with feathers, beads of shell, and other gewgaws, which they arrange very neatly in embroidery work.[7]

Since they lived on Cape Cod, an obvious landmark, the Nausets had some very early contacts with European explorers,

*Explorer Samuel de Champlain explores Massachusetts territory. Champlain was one of the first Europeans to have contact with the Nauset tribe.*

Although the Nauset would usually abandon their villages and retreat inland at the approach of a European ship, they continued to be victimized by sailors of all nationalities. In 1614 Captain Thomas Hunt captured seven Nauset and twenty Patuxet (one of whom was Squanto who later gained fame as a friend of the Pilgrims in Plymouth) and later sold them as slaves in Spain. . . . [In addition, it] appears there was a terrible sickness among Hunt's crew that was inadvertently passed to the Nauset and Wampanoag in the course of his raid.[8]

fishermen, and adventurers. Most of these meetings were less than friendly. When returning to Europe from the Caribbean, the traders passing the cape were often tempted to make extra money by kidnapping Nausets and selling them into slavery at home. Other Europeans simply stole food. Because of this history, the Nauset tribe was more hostile toward the Europeans than were their Wampanoag neighbors.

According to Lee Sultzman, who maintains the Nauset website,

## The People of the Rivers and Bays

At the time of the first contact with European explorers, the Pequot tribe was a powerful force in the coastal area between the Niantic River in Connecticut and the Weekapaug River in Rhode Island. With about sixteen thousand members, the region where the Pequots lived was one of the most densely populated in New England. The 1616–1619 epidemic did not reach the Pequots, but a 1633 smallpox epidemic reduced their numbers by 80 percent.

The Pequots established two heavily fortified villages near Mystic. In addition, there were a large number of smaller villages located along estuaries and marshes, each containing about thirty wigwams. John W. DeForest wrote about the power of the Pequots in his 1851 book *History of the Indians of Connecticut:*

> The Pequots . . . found themselves in possession of a large extent of country well adapted to their wants; but were, at the same time, completely surrounded by enemies. Their fierce spirit quailed not under this danger, and they maintained their hold on the conquered territory with a tenacity equal to the boldness with which they had seized it. They did more:

their war-parties carried terror and trembling among the numerous Narragansetts on the east, and swept with the resistless force of a tornado over the slender tribes which bordered them on the west.[9]

The Narragansetts mentioned by DeForest occupied a domain that extended throughout most of Rhode Island. Their territory also included Block Island offshore and Conanicut Island in Narragansett Bay. The powerful Narragansett sachems extended their rule over certain Nipmuc, Wampanoag, Pequot, Niantic, and Mohegan bands. The Narragansett also ruled

*A Pequot fort stands in the middle of the countryside. The Pequot people had many enemies but were fierce warriors.*

over a number of smaller sachemdoms including the Pawtuxet and Maushapogue.

The Nipmuc tribe, who numbered around ten thousand, resided in about forty villages in central Massachusetts, northern Rhode Island, and northeast Connecticut. The name originated from the Algonquian word *nipnet,* meaning "small pond place" or "freshwater people." After

epidemics and wars, only one thousand Nipmucs remained alive.

## The Mahican Tribes

The Mahican (also spelled Mohican) homeland was along the Hudson River Valley in present-day New York. The Mahicans inhabited a broad range of forested, mountainous lands that stretched between the Catskill

## The Last of the Mohicans

James Fenimore Cooper (1789–1851) was one of the first widely popular American novelists. He wrote more than fifty books, many of them dealing with patriotic themes such as the American Revolution. His series of books called the Leatherstocking Tales, about a white man named Natty Bumppo who prefers to live among Native Americans, secured his place among the great writers of the English language.

The second book of the series, *The Last of the Mohicans,* written in 1826, is an adventure set in the forest during the so-called French and Indian War (1756–1763) between Great Britain and France. The book, characterized by thrilling attacks, escapes, captures, and rescues struck a chord with Americans in the nineteenth century. It was the basis for five movies made between 1920 and 1992.

Cooper's sympathy toward Native Americans is evident in his introduction to the book.

"The Mohicans were the possessors of the country first occupied by the Europeans in this portion of the continent. They were, consequently, the first dispossessed; and the seemingly inevitable fate of all these people, who disappear before the advances, or it might be termed the inroads, of civilization, as the verdure of their native forests falls before the nipping frosts, is represented as having already befallen them. . . . The whole of that wilderness, in which the latter incidents of the legend occurred, is nearly a wilderness still, though the red man has entirely deserted this part of the state. Of all the tribes named in these pages, there exist only a few. . . . The rest have disappeared, either from the regions in which their fathers dwelt, or altogether from the earth."

Mountains and the Berkshire Hills in Massachusetts, and north to the southern end of Lake Champlain. All the Algonquian-speaking tribes that lived in this large area were classified as Mahicans, so the population numbers range as high as thirty-five thousand members. The core tribes of the Mahican confederacy near Albany, New York, numbered around eight thousand. By 1672 this had fallen to around one thousand. By the 1730s, most surviving Mahicans had migrated to western Pennsylvania and the Kankakee River Valley in Indiana. At the low point in 1796, three hundred Stockbridge, called the "Last of the Mohicans," were left alive in central Wisconsin.

Mahicans referred to themselves in their own language as *Muhhekunneuw* "people of the great river." Early Dutch explorers could not say this word so they used the Mahican word for wolf, "Manhigan," which was the name of one their most important clans. Later the English altered this to Mahican. The names have often been confused and confusing. According to researcher Lee Sultzman, who maintains a Mahican website,

It is very common for the Mohegan of the Thames River in eastern Connecticut to be confused with the Mahican from the Hudson Valley in New York (a distance of about a hundred miles). Even James Fenimore Cooper got things confused when he wrote "Last of the Mohicans" in 1826. Since Cooper lived in [central] New York and the location of his story was the upper Hudson Valley, it can be presumed he was writing about the Mahican of the Hudson River, but the spelling variation chosen (Mohican) . . . has muddled things. Other factors have contributed to the confusion. . . . [T]he Mohegan were the largest group of the Brotherton Indians in Connecticut. After the Brotherton moved to the Oneida reserve in upstate New York in 1788, they became mixed with the Stockbridge Indians (Mahican) from western Massachusetts. Because of this, the present-day Stockbridge Tribe should contain descendants from both the Mahican and Mohegan. Anyone not confused at this point may consider himself an expert.[10]

## The Lenni Lenape

South of the Mahican territories the tribes of the Lenni Lenape occupied much of what is today the state of New Jersey. Lenni Lenape has been translated to mean "men among men," and "men of our kind." After the English arrived at the Atlantic seacoast the Lenape were given a new name that was taken from Sir Thomas West, twelfth Baron De La Warre, who was the governor of the English colony at Jamestown, Virginia, in 1610. One of his colonists sailed up the Atlantic coast to the majestic bay he named in honor of his governor. In time, the Lenape people living on the shores of De La Warre Bay

*The Lenni Lenape, or Delaware Indians, occupied the area of North America that is now New Jersey.*

became known as the Delaware Indians. In the book *The Delaware Indians,* author Clinton Alfred Weslager describes the Delaware tribes and territories:

> Modern ethnologists [students of the origins of groups of people] use the terms *Delaware Indians* and *Lenni Lenapé* synonymously, and agree that the homeland of these Indians should be delimited to the states of New Jersey and Delaware, that part of southeastern Pennsylvania lying between the Susquehanna and Delaware rivers, and the southeastern part of New York

state west of the Hudson. It should not be inferred, however, that the Indian occupants of this area were closely knit political groups having a head sachem who wielded authority over a host of Indian subjects. This concept is alien to the basic structure of Delaware Indian society. . . . [Rather] each Delaware village was an independent community, having its own chieftains, and great men, who served the chieftains in the role of councilors, and participated in the decision making. Often the people living in villages along the same stream constituted what can best be described as a band, and the most influential village chief may have functioned as the nominal head of the band. The Indians and the streams on which their villages were situated were often known by the same name. For instance the natives living on . . . Rancocas Creek were called Rancocas Indians; those on the Brandywine, were known as Brandywine Indians, and so forth.[11]

The Delawares occupied a wide variety of ecological zones, from the windy marshes and coastal plains of the Atlantic Ocean to the wooded hills of Pennsylvania and the rocky terrain of northern New Jersey. As with other tribes, it is difficult to pinpoint exact population and village numbers. Historians estimate that there were about ten to twelve thousand Delawares when the Europeans arrived.

## Northeast Tribes, Populations, and Villages

The tribes of the Northeast divided themselves into a bewildering number of clans and subtribes, many of whose names and histories are no longer known. In addition, certain territories may have been claimed by more than one tribe or dominated by rival groups during different eras. In the book *Indian New England Before the Mayflower,* Howard S. Russell attempts to explain intersecting tribal locations and politics:

Beginning at what is today the New York state line, settlements of the Wappingers, related to the New York Mahicans, dotted the Long Island Sound shore. A spillover of Mahicans from the Hudson Valley later settled in the Housatonic [River] Valley in the Berkshires [in Massachusetts], and Mahicans [lived] in the Hoosic River area further north.

Easterly along the Connecticut shore resided the Western Niantics; then the powerful Pequot tribe, and their subject Mohegans, who later were to join the English in the virtual extermination of their masters. At the Rhode Island line dwelt a small tribe, the Eastern Niantics. . . .

To the north of Wampanoag territory, about southern Massachusetts Bay and Boston Harbor, a numerous tribe, the Massachusetts, people of

the Great Blue Hill, had their seats. Toward Cape Ann the domain of the Pawtuckets began, extending both north to include the lower valley of the Merrimac and its tributaries and east to the sea. To their north lived the Pennacooks. . . .

Inland, into what is now Vermont, New Hampshire, even interior Maine, the powerful Mohawks from New York to the westward had extended their influence. When recorded history began, they were collecting tribute also from the Pocumtucks in the Connecticut Valley at Deerfield and Squakeags just above them at Northfield, and south along the Connecticut River, and from the scattered and tribally unorganized Nipmuck villages in interior Massachusetts.[12]

## A Mystery for All Time

Early explorers in North America had no way of accurately counting tribal members, and experts today believe that the Europeans' estimates were far too low. Many early tallies only counted "fighting men," "bowmen," or "warriors," and left out the populations of women and children who remained largely unseen. Moreover, tens of thousands died in the early epidemics, leaving behind dozens of unoccupied villages. Later, when Puritan settlers came upon these sites, they simply guessed how many people might have lived there. Howard Russell concludes,

Considering all the data, and disregarding published estimates that appear improbable, we judge that a total of at least 60,000 natives in what are today three southern New England states and New Hampshire is not unreasonable. Vermont . . . was in the 1600s mostly unpeopled except around Vernon, Brattleboro, Newbury, and Missisquoi. . . .

The population for the entire area of what is today called New England at the time the English came may . . . have reached a total of 75,000. The precise figures we shall never know.[13]

# Chapter 2

# Villages of the Northeast Tribes

Native American tribes of the Northeast were not nomadic people. When the Europeans arrived, they were living in permanent villages and had been for many centuries. Tribes preferred to settle in scenic areas, and the forests of New England were rich in natural beauty. In 1851, John W. DeForest described the terrain in Connecticut before the forests had been cut down to make way for farms and villages:

> Connecticut [before the Europeans arrived] presents no such appearance as it exhibits now, when it was inhabited by the Pequot, the Quinnipiac, the Tunxis, and the Hammonasset. A continuous forest overspread nearly the whole landscape, adorning the hills with its verdure, darkening the valleys with its deep shadow, and bending solemnly over the margins of the rivers. No thickets choked up the way through the endless woodlands, for the underbrush was swept away every year by fires kindled for this purpose by the inhabitants. Paths led through them here and there; not paths of iron, such as those over which the steam-horse [railroad train] now flies; but winding foot-ways, along which the wild beast and the wild man alike travelled in single-file.[14]

## Native American Villages

Almost every site chosen for a village within these lush woods had to have several advantages. Villages were usually built on high elevations to grant scenic overlooks and to provide good defenses from enemy tribes. For protection from the cold northeast winter winds, a village might be built next to a sheltering hill or a thick grove of pine trees. On the other hand, in the summer, a windy spot might be desirable to blow away biting insects such as mosquitoes. A nearby supply of firewood was also advantageous.

Since water provided for transportation and a source of food, an ideal village site would be located close to the ocean, near a lake where fishing was good, or next to a confluence of two rivers. For agricultural purposes, Native Americans built their homes close to large fields or thin woods that could be easily cleared with hand tools or by burning.

Early European explorers wrote that Native American villages near Plymouth and Cape Cod were composed of separate dwellings that stood alone with no fences or other means of protection for the community. This shows that the Wampanoags and Nausets were not afraid of enemy invasion. By contrast, tribes who lived near hostile neighbors surrounded their villages with stockade fences, called palisades, made from upright trees that had been

sharpened on the ends. DeForest describes the enclosed type of village:

A part of the population, especially among the larger and more warlike tribes, seems always to have inhabited the fortified villages. These were almost invariably situated on some prominent hill, which would be easy of defense, and would command an extensive prospect by which the approach of an enemy might be perceived. The ground occupied by a village varied from a very small space up to two or three acres. The houses were closely packed together, but an open place was left in the center, which was used for amusements, for cere-

*Native Americans gather food outside their wigwam. Wigwams were one of the most common types of Indian dwelling.*

## Who Can Own the Land?

The Native American concept of land ownership, which differed completely from the European tradition, is discussed in detail in Clinton Alfred Weslager's *The Delaware Indians.*

"To the Delawares, land was like air, sunlight, or the waters of a river—a medium necessary to sustain life. The idea of an individual exclusively owning the life-giving soil was as alien to their thinking as owning the air one breathed, or the water that bubbled forth from a woodland spring. They considered plants, trees, flowers, and other natural things in the same context. An Indian once released his horses overnight in [missionary John] Heckewelder's meadow . . . and the next morning Heckewelder criticized him for so doing, to which the Indian replied,

'My friend, it seems you lay claim to the grass my horses have eaten because you had enclosed it with a fence: now tell me, who caused the grass to grow? Can you make the grass grow? . . . [T]he grass which grows out of the earth is common to all; the game in the woods is common to all. Say, did you ever eat venison and bear's meat!—"Yes, very often"—Well, and did you ever hear me or any other Indian complain about that? No; then be not disturbed at my horse having eaten only once of what you call your grass, though the grass my horses did eat, in like manner as the meat you eat, was given to the Indians by the Great Spirit.'

Land 'ownership' to the Delawares meant the right to use the land, to plant on it, to build wigwams on it, to hunt the animals that lived on it, but not to possess it permanently."

monies, for idling, and for the transaction of public business. The whole village was surrounded by a fortification, made of the trunks of young trees, firmly planted in the earth, and forming a close fence or palisade ten or twelve feet high. Where the entrance was left, the two ends of the fence overlapped each other, and made a narrow passage which was closed at night by being filled up with brushwood.[15]

## The Warmth of the Wigwam

In southern New England, Native Americans lived in wigwams. To construct this round structure the builder first marked out a circle on the ground ten to sixteen feet in diameter. Pliable saplings were embedded around the circumference every two or three feet, creating an arching roof six to eight feet high. Additional saplings were wrapped around the entire frame to give it strength, and two entrances were made about three feet in height.

The sides of the wigwam were made by women who sewed together mats made from bulrush leaves or other reeds. The women used thread from hemp, or trees that had fine inner bark. The sewing needle was made from a split rib of a deer.

The mats, about four to five feet wide and eight to ten feet long, were secured over the sapling frame and sewed to one another. For the interior walls, dried plant material woven tightly together provided considerable insulation from the cold. The entrance of the wigwam was covered with a light mat in the summer months and deerskin and bark in the winter.

Inside the wigwam, platforms ringed the sides and provided an elevated place for residents to sleep or lounge. These beds, which were wide enough for three or four people, were described by seventeenth-century writer Peter Force:

> aboute the fire [the Indians] lye upon plancks commonly aboute a foote or 18 inches above the ground raised upon railes that are borne up on forks they lay mats under them, and Coates of Deares skinnes otters beavers Racownes and of Beares

*The sapling frame of a wigwam stands ready to be covered with mats of leaves and reeds. The wigwam could house many people and was well insulated, staying warm even in cold temperatures.*

hides, all which they have dressed and converted into good leather with the haire on for their coverings and in this manner they lye as warme as they desire.[16]

In the center of each wigwam, a stone hearth provided heat and a place to cook, while a framework of green wood sticks was used to dry and smoke fish and other foods. An eighteen-inch opening in the roof allowed smoke to escape. A mat made from cord or saplings surrounded the fire hole and could be turned to prevent the wind from blowing the smoke down into the wigwam.

Wigwams were tight, comfortable dwellings capable of keeping residents warm even during the harshest New England winter. Although many Englishmen stated that the interiors of wigwams were dark, odorous, and smoky, others wrote of their solid construction, and "could testify to their being as warm as the best houses among the [English] colonists."[17]

In northern New England, the Abenaki built cone-shaped wigwams that resembled the skin-covered teepees of the western tribes. These structures—generally used in the summer—were easily rolled up and moved from campground to campground. Outside of Maine, cone-shaped wigwams were only used for temporary dwellings.

## Longhouses

While wigwams were occupied by one or two families, in the colder regions of the northeast, six or eight families—usually related—might occupy one huge shelter known as a longhouse. These dwellings were from twenty to one hundred feet long and twenty to thirty feet wide and constructed of two layers of birch or other bark over a frame of poles. The long arched roofs were punctured along the centerline with holes to permit the smoke from fires inside the house to escape.

Longhouses were most frequently used by northern and western tribes and were a necessity during long, cold New England winters. Like the wigwams, a longhouse had a sapling framework which the women covered with six- to nine-foot strips of bark from elm, chestnut, birch, or oak. These huge shingles were sewn together with thread made from pine tree roots. For roofing, reeds were tightly sewn together. The winter longhouse needed several layers of mats to keep out the snow and rain. Mats for interior walls were often decorated with geometric patterns woven into the fibers.

In 1616, Samuel de Champlain described life inside a longhouse somewhere along the coast of Maine:

On the two sides there is a kind of bench, four feet high, where they sleep in the summer to avoid the annoyance of the fleas, of which there were great numbers. In the winter they sleep on the ground on mats near the fire, so as to be warmer than they would be on the platform. They lay up a stock of dry wood, with which they fill their cabins, to burn in the winter. At the extremity of the

## Sweat Lodges

Native Americans in the northeast and elsewhere placed a great importance on the healing and cleansing powers of sweat lodges. Howard S. Russell describes the construction and use of sweat lodges in his book *Indian New England Before the Mayflower:*

"In addition to the health resources to be found in nature, the sweat bath was used as a standard cleanser, [revitalizer], and cure-all. On the shore of a clear pond or stream near their village the Indians built a circular hut. Sometimes it was partly of stones, with [a roof made of] rushes above and high enough to stand in. . . . For a floor a bed of stones was laid, and on this a fire was built. After the stones were well heated, the burning [sticks] were pushed out and the stones and any remaining coals were dowsed with water, which raised a great steam. Then the whole family—men, women, and children—would crowd in, close the opening, and sit or lie in the mist and heat. For perhaps an hour they would chat or sing while sweat poured out from every part of their bodies. At length everybody dashed out into the close-by water and swiftly cleansed the skin, then applied [plant- or animal-based] ointment to every part. Great claims are still heard for the healthful effect of sweat baths, the Finnish sauna being only one example."

*Native Americans used sweat lodges as a ritual to cleanse the body of internal and external impurities. Different forms of the sweat lodge can still be found in Indian society today.*

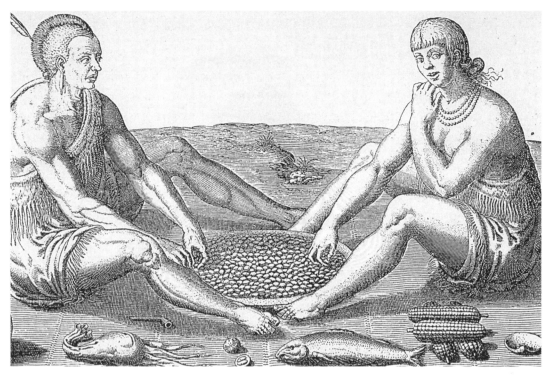

*The diet of the Northeast tribes consisted primarily of a variety of nuts and berries, fish, and some vegetables. Here, two Native Americans sit next to a bowl of corn, one of the most important foods of their diet.*

cabins there is a space, where they preserve their Indian corn, which they put into great casks made of the bark of trees and placed in the middle of their encampment. They have pieces of wood suspended, on which they put their clothes, provisions, and other things, for fear of the mice, of which there are great numbers. In one of these cabins there may be twelve fires, and twenty-four families. It smokes excessively. . . . There is no window nor any opening except that in the upper part of their cabins for smoke to escape.[18]

## Daily Necessities

Most tribal people lived outdoors when the weather permitted. But the wigwam or longhouse was a year-round storage shelter for all of a family's possessions. These material goods were mainly used for ceremony, hunting, fishing, or cooking.

Before the introduction of European trade goods, Native Americans of the northeast did not use iron or bronze, though they occasionally pounded copper into cutting tools or beads. Even without the use of metals, the tribes of the northeast were skilled artisans who were able to make whatever they needed from materials found in the forests. Howard S. Russell describes how women constructed kitchen utensils from bark:

> [A]fter the bark was painstakingly stripped from the birch tree, it was heated above the fire or by steam, then shaped for the desired vessel. Slender shoots of willow were bent to form the rim and also a handle by which the container could be hung above a fire. A large bark pail might hold as much as two or three gallons [of liquid].[19]

Women also stored a variety of other household items in woven baskets. Sewing baskets were stocked with bone and shell needles and plant threads; food baskets were filled with dried corn, acorns, and seasonings; while medicine baskets contained herbs and plant medicines. Heavy baskets woven from hemp fibers contained large tools made from bone or stone, fishing nets and lines, and other supplies.

Since ground corn was a staple of the Native American diet, every wigwam contained at least one section of tree trunk with a hollowed-out bowl in the middle. Using a slender stone shaped like a cucumber, women ground corn into flour. Other stone bowls were used for grinding nuts, seeds, and herbs.

Whatever items people could not obtain nearby, they acquired through an intricate web of trade routes that connected villages. According to *500 Nations* by Alvin M. Josephy Jr.,

In addition to local resources, most villages had long had access to valued products from other areas, carried on trails or by canoes over a network of trade routes that linked the different parts of the region. From village to village moved articles of exchange: hides and furs, wooden bowls and earthenware pots, chestnuts, berries, dried fish, and other foods, and eagerly sought white and purple beads made from certain shells by a few coastal tribes on Long Island Sound and known as wampum.[20]

## Clothing and Appearance

Native American women made beautiful clothing from plant and animal sources. Intricate designs were woven into clothing and jewelry using shell beads, porcupine quills, moose hair, and, after European traders arrived, glass beads, semiprecious stones, silver, and other items.

In 1994, author Tree Beard (Hitakonanu'laxk) of the Lenape (Delaware) tribe, wrote a book called *The Grandfathers Speak,* in which he describes the appearance and dress of his people:

> [Our] people were striking to the early Europeans. With long black hair, swarthy to near black skin, high prominent cheekbones and painted faces, sometimes with tattoos, our people were comely and handsome. We kept ourselves very

# Recording Events on Wampum

Tiny purple and white beads made from the shell of the quahog clam were called wampum, which means "strings of white" in Algonquian. Wampum was fashioned into belts and other articles that held deep spiritual value to the East Coast tribes.

Although the New England tribes had no written language, they had a rich oral tradition, and wampum was used as a memory aid to keep track of tribal history and sacred pacts between tribes. This was done through bead color and design. White beads reddened with ocher meant war. Purple beads stood for grief. White beads meant purity. A row of beads in the shape of diamonds meant friendship, while a row of beads in squares signified the council fire. The information conveyed by the wampum's design and colors was memorized by tribal wampum keepers or historians and passed from generation to generation.

To create a wampum string, an artisan clamped a fragment of seashell in a wooden vise and shaped it into a bead with a grindstone. Next, a hole was drilled in the bead with the aid of a bow drill in which the string of a small bow was pulled rapidly back and forth on a sharp stone drill. Finally the beads were strung together using a wooden loom.

Although wampum had a spiritual rather than monetary value to Native Americans, when European fur traders saw how much the Iroquois valued wampum, the white men began to use it as a form of money in trades.

clean and were very neat in dress and appearance.

Clothing was made of skins, feathers, and plant material, sewn together with thread made from [animal] sinew. Women wore dresses, men shirts, and both wore leggings, all being made from deerskin. Moccasins were also made of deerskin, and decorated with shell beads, porcupine quills, bells, etc. Men wore a loin cloth or breech clout of soft buckskin, which passes between the legs and was brought up and folded over a deerskin belt. . . . [Whereas] our Native people first dressed in deerskin clothing, after the introduction of cloth in trading [with Europeans] we started to wear cloth clothing and European-style clothing, and the whites took up our deerskin with the fringe.

Men and women wore stone and shell pendants, beads, necklaces, armbands

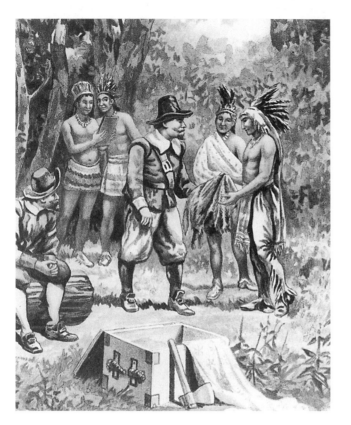

*European explorers and Native Americans trade goods with one another.*

flint, leaving a crest of long hair in the center that they made stand erect with grease. A long length of hair on an otherwise shaved head was called a scalp lock and was worn decorated with shells or other items.

Early European explorers and sailors all wore long beards and were surprised that Native American men did not. To maintain the clean-shaven look, tribesmen pulled the hair out of their faces with tweezers made of mussel shells. By 1800, however, this practice was stopped and most men had thin, wispy beards.

Men and women painted their faces using colors according to personal design, and men also painted their bodies. Women often used red paint to make spots on their cheeks and painted their ears and around the eyes.

Both sexes wore tattoos in which a design was pricked into the skin with a needle until blood was drawn. Then burnt, powdered poplar tree bark was spread upon it. The dark coloring sank into the wounds, leaving a permanent tattoo.

and anklets, and earrings of stone, shells, animal teeth and claws.

In wintertime fur robes and leggings were worn; women sometimes wore shawls made of feathers.[21]

Men and women both wore their hair long and hair was looked upon as one's connection to the Great Spirit, and a sacred signature given each person at birth by the creator. Old men let their hair grow down to their waists while young warriors shaved the sides of their heads with sharp

## Division of Labor

In daily life, Native American men and women had separate, distinct duties that were well understood. Women planted, harvested, and prepared food, gathered shellfish, collected firewood, carried water, carried supplies on journeys, cared for children, tanned hides, and made mats, baskets, and clothing. Men cut down trees, cleared the land, built wigwams, constructed dugout and birch bark canoes, built animal traps, fished, hunted, and protected their families and tribe. Older people made fishing nets, crafted clay bowls, carved stone implements, and scraped and dressed pelts for clothing.

Many early European observers recorded their incorrect impression that Native American women performed most of the hard work while the men did as little as possible. Thus, according to Governor Edward Winslow of the Plymouth Colony:

> The men employ their time wholly in hunting and other exercises of the bow, except that they sometimes take some pains at fishing. The women live a most slavish life: they carry all their burdens, set and dress their corn, gather it in, and seek out for much of their food, beat and make ready the corn to eat and have all household care lying upon them.[22]

Twentieth-century historian Howard S. Russell elaborates:

> It was [the women's] job, when the temporary shelter was to be moved, to take down the wigwam, roll up the covering mats which formed the walls, and

carry these and the poles on which they had rested to the next location. In March and April before planting started, the women gathered firewood. Daily they brought water from the spring to boil above the flame. They dug clams, caught lobsters, fished, picked berries, and "curried and suppled" . . . the skins of the game their men shot or trapped—; all in addition to cooking meals and making up clothing. They were the farmers, breaking the ground, planting the seed; cultivating, weeding,

*One of the Native American chief's duties was to become skilled with the bow and arrow so he could hunt and protect the tribe.*

*Young Native American girls learned to help their mothers with daily tasks at an early age.*

harvesting, storing the crops; and selecting seed for the season to follow. Young girls were helpers.[23]

Although women did work hard, they were also in respected positions of authority within the tribal structure. In any event, most female European settlers worked just as hard as their Native American counterparts. According to C. A. Weslager, "white women taken captive by the Delaware Indians in warfare often refused to be rescued after they had become members of an Indian community,

because they did not want to return to the subordination accorded to women in colonial society."[24]

## The Native American Family

The family unit was the center of life in the loosely knit tribal structure. Most adults married in their teens. Divorce, while rare, was a simple matter of one spouse leaving the household. Unmarried pregnancy was considered a disgrace, and young women tried to remain virgins until they were married. Most men were married to one woman, but powerful sachems, warriors, or other tribal leaders might have more than one wife.

William Penn was a prominent English Quaker and the founder of Pennsylvania. In 1683, he wrote about the family practices of the Delawares:

Of their Customs and Manners there is much to be said; I will begin with Children. So soon as they are born, they wash them in Water, and while very young, and in cold Weather . . . they Plunge them in the Rivers to harden and embolden them. . . . The Children will go [almost naked] very young, at nine moneths commonly; they wear only a small Clout round their Waste, till they are big; if Boys, they go a Fishing till ripe for the

38

Woods, which is about Fifteen; then they Hunt, and after having given some proofs of their Manhood, by a good return of Skins, they may Marry, else it is a shame to think of a Wife [until hunting skills are perfected]. The Girls stay with their Mothers, and help to Hoe the Ground, plant Corn and carry Burthens; and they do well to [get used to it] Young, [as] they must do [these things] when they are Old; for the Wives are the true Servants of their Husbands: otherwise the Men are very affectionate to them.[25]

Marriages were possible when both sets of a couple's parents gave their consent, although customs varied from tribe to tribe. Among the Abenaki, a man who wanted to marry a woman made his proposal through a friend or relative of the woman. Other times a man would give lavish gifts to the woman or her parents. Rather than staging formal weddings, couples simply began living together and other tribal members understood that they were married.

Native American women were accustomed to having babies with little assistance and often returned to their daily work within hours. Newborns were laid in soft beds of duck feathers, seeds from milkweed or cattail, or moss. In preparation for the event, the father made a smooth, flat cradle board two or three feet long to which the infant could be strapped. A soft covering was fixed to the cradle board and it could be carried on the mother's back while she moved about. If the mother was working in a garden or tanning hides, the cradle board could be hung in a nearby tree. As a child grew older and began teething, he or she was given a small bone to chew.

Native Americans treated their children with great respect and affection—they were never exposed to yelling or beatings. Children who misbehaved might be told stories of evil spirits who would harm them if they continued to be bad. Youngsters who wandered into a dangerous area of the forest might be scared off by a family member wearing a frightening mask.

Like children everywhere, play was important to Native American boys and girls. Children learned to swim at an early age and, like their parents, participated in swimming races. They pitched stones and long sticks shaped like spears, and they spun tops made from wood, stone, bone, or clay. Until the age of ten, children spent their time learning the skills of adulthood. Girls would care for dolls made from corn husks and boys would practice hunting with tiny bows and arrows. When a boy killed his first animal, the entire family joined in a celebratory feast.

Since the tribes transmitted information orally instead of in writing, children spent their nights around the fire, hearing and memorizing the history of their people. This was the school in which children learned the great accomplishments of their ancestors and the complex behaviors of animals, birds, and plants. And there were dozens of tales about spirits, giants, ghosts, and other supernatural beings.

In general, Native American people had long life spans. Before the introduction of European diseases, it was not unusual to find men and women who were sixty, seventy, or even one hundred years old. As with other Native American tribes, those of the Northeast held a deep respect for old people. According to Howard S. Russell,

> The elderly were held in honor. Where weighty themes were considered, the members of the council of elders and the subchiefs as well were called in consultation. . . . Proper consideration might take hours or even days before a decision came. The conclave might include women, for they were the . . . persons of experience and good judgment. . . . At such general sessions unanimity was the objective, and time was taken to achieve it.[26]

# Chapter 3

# The Seasons of Life

The tribes of the Northeast lived in an environment of great natural abundance. John W. DeForest listed the multitude of foods available to Native Americans in Connecticut before much of the wildlife habitat had been destroyed by cutting down forests and plowing them into farms.

> The forests were filled with animals; some of them beasts of prey, others suitable for food, others valuable on account of their furs. Flocks of wild turkeys roamed through the woods; herons fished in the marshes or along the banks of the rivers; quails, partridges, and singing birds abounded, both in the forests and open country; and, at certain times of the year, the pigeons collected in such numbers that their flight seemed to obscure the sun. The ponds, creeks and rivers swarmed with water-fowl, and various kinds of shellfish were found in profusion along the shores of the sound. The waters seemed everywhere alive with fish; and, every spring, great numbers of shad and lamprey eels ascended the rivers, furnishing a seasonable supply to the natives when their provisions were exhausted by the long and severe winter.[27]

Since the climate of the Northeast is marked by the four distinct seasons, each one brought its own blessings—and challenges—from nature. And it was the circle of the four seasons—spring, summer, autumn, and winter—that determined the patterns of work and play for the Native American tribes in the region.

## The Fresh Foods of Spring

Winters in New England are lengthy, dark, and cold. But as the days grow longer and the warming sun melts away the snow, the ice in the rivers begins to snap and break apart, and geese can be seen overhead, returning from the south.

Around mid-April, the fields, forest floors, and wetlands turn a rainbow of colors with the early flowers and herbs of spring. Native Americans took advantage of the first fresh edible greens of the season as they augmented their meals with marsh marigold, jack-in-the-pulpit, dandelion greens, and fiddlehead ferns.

In the western forests of New England, maple sugar was an important food for several inland tribes. Trees were tapped with spouts of cedar hammered into a gash in the trunk. The clear sap was collected in birch bark pails. Later the sweet maple sap was boiled down to syrup, some of it being reduced to dry sugar. The maple sugar was eaten plain, mixed with water, or sprinkled over a variety of foods as people use salt today. Hunters could survive days in the forest on a diet of dried corn meal and maple sugar mixed in water.

Springtime also meant fresh berries. Strawberries were highly valued as well as black thimbleberries, raspberries, blackberries, and blueberries that followed as the year progressed. The berries were eaten fresh, added to bread, or dried for later use. Blueberries were dried whole on frames constructed of reeds. Raspberries were cooked into a paste and spread over sheets of birch bark in the sun, where they dried into small, thin cakes which were later tied in bundles for storage.

*A maple tree is tapped for sap. Maple sap was an important part of New England tribes' diet and could be eaten in a variety of ways.*

## Fishing

Spring was also time for the tribes to gather along the waterfalls large and small to spearfish for bass, salmon, shad, and sturgeon. The fish were swimming upstream to spawn along the Merrimack, Connecticut, Maine, and lesser rivers. This was such an important activity that the Penobscot referred to April as "month of smelts," or "spearfish moon," and hostile tribes would put aside their differences to fish at a common waterfall. In addition to spears, the tribes used nets to catch fish, lighting torches at night to draw their prey into the nets.

The tribes understood that it was better to catch fish such as shad after they had spawned, to ensure the survival of the species. Thus they developed an ingenious method for catching shad only on the downstream leg of their annual migration. In the stream Native Americans would make a weir, or line of thin sticks, set close together like a picket fence, with an opening in the middle. While swimming upstream, the fish could find their way through the opening. On the return trip to the ocean, the current of the stream pushed the fish into the fencework, and Native Americans waiting on the banks could easily spear them. This method trapped so many fish that the entire tribe was needed to harvest them. Roger Williams, founder of the colony of Rhode Island, wrote, "all the neighbors, men and women, forty, fifty, a hundred, join and come in to help freely."[28]

Fish were abundant before the Europeans arrived, and DeForest lists several methods employed by the Native Americans to catch them:

They fished in various ways: with hooks, spears and nets; in canoes and along the shore; on the sea, and in the ponds and rivers. They captured, without much trouble, all the smaller kinds of fish; and, in their canoes, they often dragged the sturgeon to land with nets stoutly made of wild hemp. Sometimes porpoises got among the rocks or shallows, and afforded a glorious scene of splashing maritime warfare before they could be overpowered and dispatched. Occasionally, too, whales were thrown on shore by storms; and, being likewise killed with a great deal of effort and trouble, yielded a new variety, and an abundant supply, of food to the inhabitants. Fish were then far more plentiful than at the present time. . . . Even the Indian children would then take them, by wading out into the flats and shallows, and spearing them with a pointed stick as they swam fearlessly by.[29]

Although fishing was better in the spring, it was also a year-round activity. Seventeenth-century writer William Wood was surprised to find the natives cutting round holes in the ice in the winter "about which they sit in their naked breeches, catching of Pikes, Pearches, Breames, and other sorts of freshwater fish."[30]

In the summer, low water in the streams allowed tribes to construct stone walls along the streambed in the shape of a funnel where the streambed dropped. This created rapids that would cause fish to tumble out of the water into sieves of sticks placed at the open end of the wall.

## The Native American Garden

While Native American men were off fishing, women began planning for their

# Dugout and Birch Bark Canoes

When Europeans first came to North America, they were amazed by the agile canoes the Native Americans used to travel on water. Dugout canoes started out as pine logs about eighteen inches wide and twenty feet long. Men used hot coals, shell scrapers, and stone axes to dig out a passenger compartment.

Birch bark canoes were lighter and even more nimble. These canoes were constructed of the bark of giant, ancient birch trees which were cut in the winter when the bark was hardest and toughest. The process of canoe construction was described by William A. Haviland and Marjory W. Power in *The Original Vermonters.*

"First a large tree, two feet in diameter and knot-free for a length of twenty-two feet, was felled so as to lie across two other logs. A slow fire was built beneath to keep the bark pliable, which was slit and peeled off with a chisel of fire-hardened wood. The bark was placed on the ground, outside up, and inside rails of spruce or birch wood were sewn with spruce root to the two edges of the bark. Following this, logs and rocks were placed on the bark, which was then shaped by raising the sides and driving stakes all around the outside to hold things in place. As the bark was shaped, slits were cut as necessary, at the two ends, and cross pieces of larch or maple were sewn in place between the rails. The entire inside of the

bark was coated with pitch, and then lined with strips of cedar shaved to a thickness of less than 1/2 inch. Any leaks were plugged with spruce gum."

It took three weeks to build a canoe that would last about ten years and carry up to six hundred pounds. Canoe building was one of the most important and extensively cultivated skills practiced by northeast tribes, and it furnished an easy mode of travel—without which the lives of the Native Americans would have been greatly restricted.

*Indian tribes everywhere built canoes. Canoes were very functional and one of the quickest ways for Native peoples to travel.*

*Although Native Americans did not raise farm animals, they did raise and keep dogs. Dogs were used to hunt, retrieve, and warn villagers of strangers.*

summer gardens. Tender young corn and bean sprouts are easily ruined by frost, so planting only began when the budding leaves of the oak tree were as large as the ear of a squirrel—around late April or early May. Before this work was done, however, weeds and stalks that remained in the fields from the previous season were gathered and burned in the field, providing potash and other nutrients for the next crop.

In summer 1605, Champlain wrote about the Native American agricultural practices he observed along the coast of Maine:

We saw their Indian corn, which they raise in gardens. Planting three or four kernels in one place, they then heap up about it a quantity of earth with [shell of the horseshoe crab]. . . . Then three feet distant they plant as much more, and thus in succession. With this corn they put in each hill three or four [kidney] beans, which are of different colors.

## Tobacco

To the Abenaki, tobacco was a sacred plant that symbolized the "breath of life." Smoking the leaves created a social bond between people, and invitations to a ceremony were offered with a pinch of tobacco. Tribes formalized peace treaties with the communal smoking of tobacco and herbs. Important occasions warranted the use of a long, ornate pipe called a calumet, which had a feather-decorated pipe stem and an intricately carved bowl.

Europeans were introduced to tobacco by Native Americans in the sixteenth century. In 1535, explorer Jacques Cartier attempted to smoke with Native Americans. His observations were recorded in *Voyages of Samuel de Champlain 1604-1618.*

"They fill their bodies full of smoke, till that it commeth out of their mouth and nostrils, even as out of the [tunnel] of a chimney. They say that this doth keepe them warme and in health; they never goe without some of it about them. We ourselves have tryed the same smoke, and having put it in our mouthes, it seemed almost as hot as pepper."

Tobacco was also used for medicinal purposes. Native Americans used it to treat toothaches and as a painkiller. They apparently believed that it had antiseptic properties as well.

Smoking is an addictive habit; and, when explorers took tobacco back to Europe, its use spread rapidly. Sir Walter Raleigh popularized pipe smoking in Great Britain in 1586, and the consumption of tobacco spread with each voyage of discovery from Europe. Tobacco, the first profitable crop exported from America to Europe, ensured the prosperity and success of the colonies on North American shores.

After the corn and beans were planted, women brought two or three fish from the weirs in the river and placed them at the base of each hill, covering them with soil. This provided fertilizer for each plant. When the beans grew up, the French explorer continued, they would twine around

the corn, which reaches to the height of from five to six feet; and they

keep the ground very free from weeds. We saw there many squashes, and pumpkins, and tobacco, which they likewise cultivate.[31]

As with gardens anywhere in the world, crop-eating pests were often a problem. Native Americans had to ward off raccoons, woodchucks, deer, moose, and even bears, who could systematically strip a ripening cornfield in one night. To keep birds out of their gardens, some gardeners soaked crop seeds in hellebore, a plant-based drug, and distributed them between the rows of corn. When birds ate these seeds they became dizzy and appeared drunk. This strange behavior frightened other birds away. In addition to this method, children sometimes trained hawks to guard the fields and chase off crop-eating birds.

Although they were skilled farmers, Native Americans did not keep domestic farm animals. Each village, however, was well supplied with dozens of dogs. Depending on the family's standing in the community, a wigwam might be home to six or more dogs. These dogs were thin, with fox-like heads and bodies resembling wolves. Most were trained to obey a low voice command or a signal from a master's hand. Dogs were used to hunt, retrieve, and warn villagers that strangers were nearby. Dog meat was not normally eaten but on a special occasion a favorite dog might be sacrificed for an honored guest.

## Celebrating Nature's Bounty in Autumn

As the days grew long and the summer sun climbed high in the sky, women spent the cool mornings chopping the weeds between the cornrows with a stone-tipped hoe. During the corn-growing period, people went to the rivers to fish and into the forests to dig for roots and herbs.

By August, the Native American family was dining daily on summer squash and early beans. As the corn silks darkened, the tribes prepared for the Green Corn Feast. This week-long ceremony was marked by dancing, songs of thanksgiving, and nightly feasting on the early milky kernels of summer corn.

The very first kernels were not eaten, however, but ceremoniously presented in a pot to the spirit powers. This offering was then burned to cinders, prayers were recited, and new corn was roasted over the fire for the hungry people. As children husked the fresh corn, they saved the silk to use as a flavoring in the next winter's stews.

As the days passed, more corn ripened. To preserve it for later use, some of the ears were boiled or parched in a hot fire. The kernels were then sliced from the cob, dried in the sun, and stored. Later, during the long stormy days of autumn when it was difficult to leave the wigwam, women and girls would grind the dried kernels into meal.

When the nights grew chilly in September, beans were pulled and dried for storage, while squash and pumpkins were taken from the fields, sliced in half, and dried in the sun. Mature corn, which is not hurt by light frost, remained in the fields. Women selected the best-looking ears to keep for seed, pulling back the husks to let them dry on the plant. These ears would later be braided into a beautiful rope that was suspended from the rafters of the longhouse or wigwam. Hung in this way, seed corn remained vital for several years. The rest of the corn was harvested and dried on mats for later use.

Excess corn was stored in a variety of ways to remain useful for the entire winter. Native Americans in Massachusetts put their corn and other grains into large grass sacks, which they buried in sand.

Before the first snows of winter began to fall, children harvested the bitter beach

## Modern Foods Received from Native Americans

The unspoiled northeast American wilderness provided a rich and varied diet to the Native Americans who lived there. In the book *Indian New England Before the Mayflower,* Howard S. Russell lists dozens of foods that were used by Native Americans—many of them totally new to European settlers.

*Cereal Foods*
Berry cake
Corn bread
Corn chowder
Corn fritters
Hominy
Hulled corn
Johnnycake
Nut bread
Squash bread

*Fowl and Flesh*
Roast turkey and other local wild game birds and animals of wide variety

*Fruits and Nuts*
Beach plums [native to sandy Cape Cod]
Blackberries
Blueberries
Cranberries
Elderberries
Gooseberries
Grapes

Raspberries (black and red)
Strawberries
Watermelon
Beechnuts
Chestnuts
Hickorynuts

*Vegetables*
Beans, baked or boiled
Bean soup
Green corn
Pumpkin, baked, boiled
Squash, baked, boiled
Succotash

*Sea Food*
Baked bluefish
Clams, baked, steamed
Clam chowder
Cod
Crabs
Fish chowder
Halibut
Herring
Lobsters, baked, broiled, boiled
Oysters, raw, escalloped, stewed
Salmon, boiled, broiled, planked, smoked
Shad
Smelts
Swordfish and many local varieties

plum and cranberries from the marshes. The trees were heavy with their nutritious yields of beechnuts, chestnuts, walnuts, and acorns, which were picked and stored. "If the squirrels [ate the nuts first] the family could later eat the squirrels, as well as the bears, who were also fond of nuts."[32]

## The Fall Hunt

During harvest time, women, men, and children all helped prepare and preserve food for the coming winter. After the crops were in, the men and boys left for the autumn hunt. Cold days were best for hunting, since in warm or moderate temperatures the flesh of the slaughtered animals would spoil before it could be transferred back to the village.

While Europeans were accustomed to dividing and subdividing land into individual parcels, Native Americans hunted in vast stretches of unoccupied forest. C. A. Weslager describes how the Delaware tribes shared their hunting territories:

> Among the Delawares there existed family hunting territories consisting of parcels of wooded land of various sizes, bounded by streams, the seashore, or other natural landmarks, usually known by designated names.
> . . .
> These hunting territories were not necessarily contiguous to the villages where the owners resided, and in many instances they were some distance away. This is consistent with

the Delawares' custom of seasonally leaving their villages to hunt, each group of families pursuing game on their respective territories.[33]

Native Americans hunted with spears, bolas, and bows and arrows. Knives and arrow points were made from flint. And as Lenape author Tree Beard states: "[Flint] is sharper than the finest steel, and so a flint knife is not perhaps as primitive or inferior as one might think."[34]

The first animals hunted in autumn were ducks and geese that were settled in the darkness of early morning on rivers, marshes, and other smooth water. Native American hunters drifted quietly in their canoes, then suddenly lit torches to cause confusion among the birds. In the first few seconds after the torches were lit, the waterfowl scrambled about, trying to take off, while the men hit them with canoe paddles or clubs. Specially trained dogs jumped in the water to retrieve the game.

Later in the season, hunters walked to grassy fields where deer and moose browsed on grass and bears found acres of blueberries. Without the benefit of horses, the men gathered in long lines to drive the deer to a narrow point between trees, where they made easy targets for the hunters waiting with bows and arrows. Meat which was not eaten right away was dried at a nearby camp over a fire. Skins, sinew, and bone were saved for their many uses.

In 1774 missionary John Heckewelder, who traveled extensively among native tribes, wrote about the hunting experience:

The hunter prefers going out . . . on an empty stomach; he says, that hunger stimulates him to exertion by reminding him continually of his wants, whereas a full stomach makes a hunter easy, careless, and lazy, ever thinking of his home and losing his time to no purpose. With all their industry, nevertheless . . . many a day passes over their heads that they have not met with any kind of game, nor consequently tasted a morsel of victuals; still they go on with their chase, in hopes of being able to carry some provisions home, and do not give up the pursuit until it is so dark that they can see no longer.

The morning and evening, they say, are the precious hours for the hunter. They lose nothing by sleeping in the middle of the day, that is to say, between ten o'clock in the morning and four in the afternoon, except in dark, cloudy, and rainy weather, when the whole day is nearly equally good for hunting.[35]

As autumn deepened and the first snows began to fall, it became easier to track game through the forests because of their trails in the snow. By the time the bitter winter lay on the land, the hunters were once again snug and warm in their wigwams and longhouses eating deer, moose, and bear jerky next to the hearth.

Tribes such as the Abenaki lived too far north to grow crops, forcing them to rely on hunting all winter long. In 1606, Champlain described the winter hunting practices along the far northern coast of present-day Quebec when temperatures dipped well below zero degrees Fahrenheit:

During the winter, in the deepest snows, they hunt elks and other animals, on which they live most of the time. And, unless the snow is deep, they scarcely get rewarded for their pains, since they cannot capture anything except by a very great effort, which is the reason for their enduring and suffering much. . . . They clothe themselves in winter with good furs of beaver and elk. . . . When they go a hunting, they use a kind of snowshoe twice as large as those hereabouts, which they attach to the soles of their feet, and walk thus over the snow without sinking in, the women and children as well as the men.

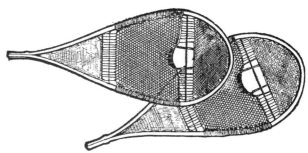

*The snowshoe was commonly used to make hunting easier for Native Americans during the winter months.*

They search for the track of animals, which, having found, they follow until they get sight of the creature, when they shoot at it with their bows, or kill it by means of daggers attached to the end of a short pike, which is very easily done, as the animals cannot walk on the snow without sinking in. Then the women and children come up, erect a hut, and they give themselves to feasting.[36]

## Shellfish

For the Woodland tribes of the Northeast, seafood was the most dependable day-to-day food available. In the fall, villagers would gather in great numbers to dry seafood in the sunshine or on a frame over a smoky fire to discourage flies. Great quantities of lobster, crab, oysters, and clams were preserved in this way to be used as a mainstay of the winter diet.

Evidence of this abundance of seafood may be seen in the huge piles of empty shells left behind by the Native Americans. Called clam banks, these piles of waste took up twenty-four acres on the Connecticut shore at Milford. Scores of clam banks have been identified along Narragansett Bay, in Cape Cod, and in Maine. Some still exist that are three feet deep and ten to twenty acres in size.

To cook shellfish, Native Americans held clambakes in which rocks were heated in a roaring fire. When the wood

*Early Native Americans left these oyster shell mounds. The mounds of various seashells found throughout Northeast coastal America are a reminder of the great quantities of shellfish Indians consumed.*

had burned down, the embers were scraped away and clams, fish, and green corn were placed on the hot rocks. Seaweed was piled on the rocks, sending forth great clouds of steam. After a time, the food was pulled from the rocks and the village gathered for a feast.

## A Winter's Day in the Wigwam

In the deepest depths of winter, families spent long days in their wigwams. The winds howling from the northeast blew snow between the brown rows of dead cornstalks. Inside the wigwams it got cold at night. As dawn broke, boys laced up their moccasins, tied deerskins around their ears, and went out to fetch armfuls of stored firewood. Girls were sent out with pails to collect water from holes in nearby streams. The father might go out to check traps set the previous evening. The mother would begin preparing breakfast, maybe cutting up red squirrels killed the day before and cooking them in a stew pot with some dried corn, beans, and chestnuts. Later, the family would gather round the hearth to scoop the stew into bowls with shells gathered at last summer's trip to the beach.

If the day was dark and stormy, the mother and daughters would spend the afternoon grinding corn, repairing clothes, and doing beadwork by the firelight. Father and sons might work on burls of oak that were cut during the fall. By laying white-hot pebbles on the burls, rubbing sand onto the surfaces, and scraping them with a beaver's tooth, these burls were slowly transformed into soup bowls. Bear fat was rubbed into the final product while the mother prepared corn cakes for dinner.

As night fell, relatives might arrive, having walked over on snowshoes from their nearby wigwam. Then the men would light their pipes and tell stories of heroes, spirits, and monsters. Finally the children would fall asleep before the fire with tales of ancient legends coloring their dreams.

# Chapter 4

# Spirits and Healing Powers

From the frozen forests of Maine and Quebec to the sandy shores of Long Island, Native Americans of the Northeast were deeply spiritual people who cherished their ancient religious beliefs. To these tribes the water, sun, moon, skies, winds, plants, rocks, and animals were all alive with gods and goddesses. These deities were able to bestow blessings—or wreak havoc—depending on dozens of signs and omens.

Native Americans paid homage to their deities in many different ritual feasts and dances. These were held at certain times throughout the year such as in early spring, in summer when the corn ripened, and during midwinter. Sachems were the hosts of these seasonal rituals, marked by chanted prayers, rhythmic drumming, elaborate costumes, frenzied dancing, and feasting.

Religious rites were also held during milestones in an individual's life: the naming of a baby, the attainment of puberty, marriage, and death. Other rituals and rites were performed in the event of misfortunes such as sickness, drought, famine, and war.

Behind the rituals, Native Americans in New England held a deep respect for nature, for it was within nature that their gods and goddesses existed. Because of these beliefs, Native Americans thought it was a sin to injure any creature without good reason—for example, to provide food for people. Similarly, the Native Americans were careful not to deplete the supply of edible plants:

Every man, bird, beast, flower, fruit, or even rock had its role and special value as a part of [the] whole. Hence it deserved respect and, if used by man, appreciation. If the muskrat's store of lily roots was raided [for example], the [people who took it] must never take all but must leave sufficient to carry the muskrat family to the next season. The muskrats had gathered the roots: they were entitled

*Native Americans gather around the fire for a ritual dance. Dances and feasts were an important part of Native American spiritual culture.*

## Creation Beliefs

All cultures from every part of the world contain creation stories about how humans came to be. Although different North American tribes held various creation beliefs, many were similar to those of the Delawares. The "Turtle Island" belief holds that the world was created on the back of a giant turtle. This legend, passed down from generation to generation, states that in the beginning there was water everywhere. The Creator brought up a turtle from the depths of the sea, and as the water splashed from his back, a tree took root on it. The tree sent out a sprout and became a man.

to a living. If the bark of a white birch was taken for a canoe, the tree received thanks, perhaps a gift of tobacco and an apology. . . .

So the bones of the beaver with whose flesh the family had satisfied their hunger and whose fur would help warm their bodies must not be thrown carelessly to the dogs but returned to the animal's native stream. . . . Any waste of the meat of bear, deer, even chipmunk would have been an offense to the slain animal.[37]

A second sprout appeared, and this was a woman. The Delawares believed that they were descendants of this couple. The turtle became a highly respected symbol of Mother Earth, and it was believed that the ebb and flow of the tides was caused by the turtle breathing.

Further to the north, tribes such as the Narragansetts and Wampanoags believed in many deities they called manitous. The chief manitou was named Cautantowit, also known by various Algonquian tribes as Kiehtan or Woonand.

Cautantowit figures into the Narragansett creation belief: When the earth was very young, evil spirits released a great flood. Some animals escaped drowning by fleeing to a tall mountain in the Southwest where Cautantowit lived. The birds and animals who lived around Cautantowit's mountain house had many godlike qualities from association with the great being.

Cautantowit set about remaking the mudsoaked earth after the flood had receded. He made a man and woman from stone but was unhappy with the result. He smashed the statues and fashioned a man and a woman from a living tree. This second couple proved satisfactory, so the manitou gave these first humans immortal souls. To help these people, Cautantowit gave them rules for living, along with corn and beans from his garden. All of the Narragansett were believed to be children of these first two humans. If they were good, and made the most of their lives by practicing wisdom,

## Interpreting Native American Legends

In spite of their dramatic defeats at the hands of the Europeans in the seventeenth century, Native American communities survived this stressful period and some remain intact today. According to William S. Simmons in *Spirit of the New England Tribes,* although Native American culture was practically destroyed by the Europeans,

"a continuous tradition of beliefs and legends has lived in [Indians'] imaginations, and much of it has been recorded over the years. This is not to say that the oral traditions of twentieth-century persons of Indian descent are identical with those of their prehistoric ancestors, for most of their aboriginal folklore has died out, changed, or been infused with borrowings from the majority culture. Nevertheless, their oral narratives show [a strong connection] with [their ancient] traditions."

Simmons goes on to explain that much that has been written about Native American beliefs is based on source material prepared by Europeans.

"In most cases, whites [wrote] the texts, particularly in the early years. Whites may have heard the narratives directly from Indians, but when they retold the narratives or wrote them down they often introduced unconscious bias and conscious embellishments that interfered with the Indian voice. A few collectors . . . presented Indian narrative materials in a way that respected the words of the Indian speakers. Too many others . . . buried Indian contributions beneath their own literary improvisations."

In spite of such limitations, the oral traditions and Native American legends have survived into the twenty-first century and still have much to teach about the ancient beliefs of the first Americans.

valor, and strength, they could go to Cautantowit's house when they died. There all their needs would be taken care of. On the other hand, evil people, thieves, and murderers would restlessly wander, hungry and tired throughout eternity.

In 1624, Governor Edward Winslow of the Plymouth Colony wrote down the Wampanoag beliefs concerning Cautantowit:

> [They] say there is no sachim or king, but Kiehtan [Cautantowit] who dwelleth above in the heavens, whither all good men go when they die, to see their friends, and have their fill of all things. This his habitation lieth far westward in the heavens, they say: thither the bad men go also, and knock on his door, but he bids them . . . that they wander in restless want and penury [poverty]. Never man saw this Kiehtan; only old men tell them of him, and bid them tell their children, yea to charge them to teach their posterities [children] the same. . . . This power [of Kiehtan] they acknowledge to be good; and . . . they . . . meet together and cry unto him; and so likewise for plenty, victory, etc., sing, dance, feast, give thanks, and hang up garlands and other things in memory of him.[38]

Cautantowit was a wise god who never meddled in the day-to-day affairs of people. The living never saw him in dreams or visions. In fact, even though people communicated with him through sacrifice,

prayers, and praise, Cautantowit remained in the afterworld with the souls of the dead.

## Hobbamocko, the Evil Manitou

Much more visible in the lives of Native Americans was the manitou of evil called Hobbamocko (also spelled Hobbamock and Hobbamoqui), whose name was related to the Algonquian words for death and the cold northeast wind. Hobbamocko was responsible for human plagues and calamities. He was associated with the color black and the Native Americans imagined that they saw him most often at night in the shapes of Englishmen "in the most hideous woods and swamps."[39]

Out of fear for his awesome malignant power, Hobbamocko received veneration and many prayers. Rituals were held for him to appease his wrath.

Some tribal members, called *pniese*, obtained clear visions of Hobbamocko in dreams or visions. To inspire these visions, a *pniese* would undergo a difficult ritual that involved staying awake for days, fasting, and taking hallucinogenic drugs which included a nausea-producing, opium-like drug from the hellebore plant.

Those chosen to be *pniese* were usually boys on the brink of puberty. The long, difficult ordeal involved cycles of drinking and vomiting bitter herbs until, according to Winslow,

> by reason of faintness, they can scarce stand on their legs, and then must go forth into the cold. . . .

## The Quest for a Guiding Vision

By the time young Native American boys and girls reached puberty they were anxious to seek out a vision or special dream that would in some way define their personality. This search was called a vision quest and it was a common practice among Native Americans of the Northeast and elsewhere. Tree Beard explains the Lenape, or Delaware, vision quest in *The Grandfathers Speak.*

"The most important spiritual undertaking of our people is the vision quest, or *linkwe-hèlan.* Our young men, when they are 14 or 15 years old, make preparations for a fasting quest, alone in the forest, undergoing prior purification, and praying for a vision. We believe that a man is nothing without a vision. Until one has a vision one merely exists; but having a vision brings one alive, giving meaningful purpose and direction to one's life. Upon receiving a vision, we then seek to fulfill this. Now, we believe that women are naturally fulfilled in their purpose, that is to have children, to raise and nurture them, and thus they don't really need to seek a vision. However, if a woman feels the need to or desire to, she may also seek for a vision on a fasting quest. . . . The vision quest guides a person to their path in life, teaches them their duty before the Creator, gives them medicines to protect, help and guide them, gives them Guardian Spirit(s), and blesses them with a sacred name. The vision quest is most important, for it gives us a sense of who we are, makes us aware of the purpose of our lives, and gives us greater understanding of all that exists around us, and our place in the Circle of Life."

[Shamans] beat their shins with sticks, and cause them to run through the bushes, stumps, and brambles, to make them hardy and acceptable to the devil, that in time he may appear unto them.[40]

This arduous procedure of purification and toughening was supposed to give the new *pniese* standing to bargain with Hobbamocko, requesting, for example, to be made impervious to knives, arrows, and hatchets while in battle. After the harsh ordeal, the *pniese* became a counselor to sachems, participated in tribal decisions concerning war, and collected tribute from the sachems' subjects. He also became a respected warrior who would charge fearlessly into battle, convinced of Hobbamocko's protection against death.

## A Wide Array of Manitous

Not all manitous were as unknowable as Cautantowit or as difficult to bargain with as Hobbamocko. On earth, all good luck and blessings came from the animals that lived around Cautantowit's home. The spirits of these individual manitous were adopted by Native Americans as personal guardians. These animal

*A group of Native Americans gathers around a fire, where they called upon their deities for blessings.*

spirits were among a wide array of other manitous.

The Narragansetts repeated to Roger Williams the names of thirty-seven of these [manitous], each being an object of worship, and each bearing a significant name. There was a god of the north, a god of the south, a god of the east, a god of the west, a god of the house, a god of women, and a god of children. The sun, the moon, the sea, the fire, and many other things were believed to be animated by spirits; and each of them, as circumstances seemed to require, might be made an object of sacrifice and adoration. Roger Williams [himself a clergyman] once disputed some Narragansetts about the existence of Yotaanit, their god of fire. To his arguments they replied: "What! is it possible that this fire is not a divinity? It comes out of a cold stone; it saves us from dying of hunger; if a single spark falls into the dry wood it consumes the whole country. Can anything which is so powerful be other than a deity?"[41]

Native Americans had day-to-day relationships with their personal deities. At times, the manitous would reveal themselves through dreams, visions, or mysterious sights and sounds in the forest. Other times the manitous were called up to inspire strength and wisdom. In a mythical cycle, these spirits, in their supernatural dimensions, were the bond between humans, creatures of the earth, and the great manitou Cautantowit.

The worlds of Native American spirituality were strange and confusing to early Europeans, and they remain a mystery to many today. In *The Grandfathers Speak,* Tree Beard attempts to explain:

All of these different worlds, or circles of being, are here altogether within and behind each other, occupying the same space, together making a whole. One may compare them to an onion, composed of its many layers, circles within circles making up the whole, and you will be as close to a true understanding as is possible for our merely human minds.[42]

## The Power of the Powwows

Native American spiritual leaders who understood the complicated world of manitous and who could communicate with the spirits were known as powwows (also called pawwaws or powachs). In modern times, the word powwow is used to describe an event where Native Americans gather together to dance, sing, pray, play, socialize, and feast. In the seventeenth century this Algonquian word was used to describe an individual who was a shaman or a medicine man.

These powerful individuals, usually men, specialized in a variety of spiritual and worldly duties known as medicine. According to Tree Beard,

## Ghosts, Giants, and Elves

In addition to manitous, Native American beliefs are rich with stories about ghosts, witches, giants, little people, and supernatural warriors. Tradition among the Wampanoag states that the first Native Americans to populate Martha's Vineyard met a giant named Maushop, who could eat an entire whale during one meal. He created many of the landmarks and rock formations along the rocky coast and protected the Native Americans from a giant, human-eating bird. Unfortunately, when the English arrived, Maushop departed, leaving behind nothing but the coastal fog, which was believed to be smoke from his pipe.

In the north, tribes such as the Penobscot of Maine and eastern Canada believed in their own giant named Glooskap (or Gluskap) who created the first Native Americans. In the beginning Glooskap created Mikumwess, who were small elves, or little men who dwelt among the rocks. Glooskap then shot his arrow into an ash tree and humans came out of the bark. The giant Glooskap next created animals, but he made them very large. According to *Glooskap's Children*, by Peter Anastas,

"Then he said to the great Moose who was as tall as a giant, 'What would you do should you see an Indian coming?' The Moose replied, 'I would tear down the trees on him.' Then Glooskap saw that the Moose was too strong and made him smaller so that the Indians could hunt him. Then he said to the Squirrel, who was the size of a Wolf, 'What would you do if you should meet an Indian?' And the Squirrel answered, 'I would scratch down trees on him.' Then Glooskap said, 'You are too strong.' And he took the Squirrel in his hands and smoothed him down, and he made him little."

There are several ways that one might be guided onto the path of medicine, as a prophet, a healer, a seer, a sweatlodge doctor, an herbalist, a pipe carrier, one who works with fire, etc. . . . Often medicine people are specialized in a certain area, for example in locating missing or lost persons or objects, or they may be gifted in two or more areas.[43]

Powwows led the ceremonial rituals that were performed throughout the year, such as the harvest festivals and midwinter festivals. They employed a variety of wild body movements, costumes, magic, and tricks to impress the other tribe members and call forth the spirits. In 1643, Puritan leader Roger Williams wrote about a medicine man leading the tribe in worship:

[The powwows] doe begin and order their services, and Invocation of their Gods, and all the people follow, and joyne interchangeably in a laborious bodily service, unto sweatings, especially of the Priest, who spends himselfe in strange Antick Gestures, and Actions even unto fainting.[44]

A shaman sometimes put on a grotesque mask and dressed up as a fearful bird, a wild beast, or a legendary monster. When performing his duties, a shaman danced and gesticulated violently while howling, singing, and shouting. Tricks and illusions were also utilized. Some shamans could stab a knife into the air and bring it down covered in blood; others would cut off a sick person's hair, turn it into a supposedly magic arrow, and shoot it back at the patient to cure him. Still other shamans specialized in a form of clairvoyance and prophecy called divination.

As diviners, the shamans determined the causes and outcome of events in the past, future, and at a distance by conjuring visions which they read as good or bad omens, by direct encounters with external spirits and by the insight provided by their own guardian spirits. In addition to providing answers to questions about illness, war, and politics, they also identified thieves and murderers.[45]

It is believed that a divination rite was held when the Pilgrims first landed in Massachusetts. The Native Americans refused to approach the intruders for several weeks. Instead a group of shamans from all over the area met, possibly to divine the best course for dealing with their new neighbors. Pilgrim leader William Bradford wrote about the powwows' ceremony that preceded the Native leader's approach to the English:

*A shaman would often dress in costume by wearing masks or elaborate clothes when performing his duties.*

[Before] they came to the English to make friendship, they gott all the Powachs [powwows] of the cuntrie, for 3. days togeather, in a horid and divellish maner to curse and execrate [the English] with their conjurations, which assembly and service they held in a darke and dismale swampe.[46]

## Bewitching Enemies

Powwows claimed to be able to use their personal power to bewitch enemies and rivals for their own ends or for patrons who employed them for a fee. One technique for such activities has been described as "magical intrusion," which involved enchanting an object, such as an arrowhead, a bone, or even a hair, that could project into a victim's body to kill him. This was accomplished by invoking a spirit in "the real body of a Serpent, which comes directly towards the [victim] in the house or in the field . . . and do shoot the bone (as they say) into the Indian's body."[47]

In addition to bewitching enemies, powwows were called upon when misfortune struck. Powwows generally believed that calamity occurred either because the Great Spirit was angry, in which case nothing could be done, or because an enemy shaman had pronounced a curse. The second cause could be fixed, usually by bargaining with Hobbamocko to help. If the cure for the illness or disaster did not work, the shaman simply stated that Cautantowit was angry and could not be appeased.

Despite reports that native sorcery prevented English dogs from barking at Na-

tive Americans, the English people were not very afraid of shamans, whom they considered "weake witches."[48] The Native Americans, on the other hand, were afraid that the colonists were cursing them and blamed English sorcery for the plagues of diseases that decimated their tribes.

## Medicine and Healing

A shaman's job involved more than placing curses on people or dogs. Shamans were also called medicine men; and, when people became ill, it was the shaman who was called in to heal them, often using herbs as medicine. Champlain wrote: "The [herbs] that grew in the woods were the source from which their pharmacy was supplied. There was healing in the trees."[49]

Healing rituals could last for several hours, and were usually attended by a large audience of friends and family members. In 1624, Edward Winslow attended one such medical rite:

[We] found the house so full of men, as we could scarce get in. . . . There were they in the midst of their charms for [the sick man], making such a hellish noise, as it [sickened] us that were well, and therefore unlike to ease him that was sick. About him were six to eight women, who [rubbed] his arms, legs, and thighs, to keep heat in him.[50]

As Winslow watched, the powwow began a musical invocation and the audience joined in like a choir. The gestures of the powwow were said to be fierce, odd, and laborious; the powwow performed them until he sweated and foamed. In 1634, William Wood described this process:

> [The] powwow . . . proceeds in his invocations, sometimes roaring like a bear, other times groaning like a dying horse, foaming at the mouth like a chased boar, smiting his naked breast and thighs with such violence as if he were mad. Thus will he continue sometimes half a day, spending his lungs, sweating out his fat, and tormenting his body in this diabolical worship.[51]

In addition to the wild shamanic dances, medicine men also laid hands on sick people, sucking out poisons or splinters, dressing wounds, and administering healing

*A medicine man prepares a potion for his patient. Medicine men were greatly respected in Native American society and sometimes drew crowds of spectators.*

## Native American Medicine Then and Now

Native American healers were intimately familiar with the medicinal uses of herbs and plants. And modern science has proven the value of many of these ancient Native American remedies. Francis Jennings makes mention of this in *The Invasion of America.*

"[French explorer Jacques] Cartier learned and used an Indian cure for [the vitamin-deficiency disease called] scurvy, but Europe forgot the lesson and continued to endure the disease until a British naval surgeon read Cartier's account two centuries later. Indians [also] did the 'pharmaceutical spadework' that led to the discovery of insulin, as acknowledged by the discoverer. Modern obstetricians have learned—but only since World War II—the superiority of Indian [birthing] practices to European (and childbirth was the great killer of Europe's women). The Indians used American foxglove as a [heart] stimulant for centuries before [a drug from foxglove called] digitalis was discovered in England. . . .

Only a handful of indigenous vegetable drugs known to science today were not used by aboriginal Indians, and the Indian usages generally corresponded with modern approved practice. . . . [Although] Indian herbalism was not a science, seventeenth-century European medicine was not much of a science either. The [shortness] of European life expectations in that era is confirmation enough."

herbs and potions. John Heckewelder had great respect for Native American herbal doctors and their cures:

I must say that their practice in general succeeds pretty well. I have myself been benefited and cured by taking their . . . medicines in fevers, and by being sweated in their manner while labouring under stubborn rheumatism. . . . They are also well skilled in curing wounds and bruises. I once for two days and two nights suffered the most excruciating pain from [an inflamma-tion] on one of my fingers. . . . I had recourse to an Indian woman, who in less than half an hour relieved me entirely by a simple . . . poultice made of the root of the common blue violet. . . . I firmly believe that there is no wound, unless it is absolutely mortal . . . which an Indian surgeon . . . will not succeed in healing.[52]

## Death Among the Lenape

As in every other society, Native Americans practiced elaborate death rituals when the medicines of the shamans failed to cure the sick. When a person lay near death, women of the family blackened their faces with soot or charcoal. When the person died, men also blackened their faces in sorrow. A door or window was opened a crack to allow the spirit of the deceased to travel on to Cautantowit's home. Lenape author Tree Beard wrote about the soul after death:

> In our view of life, we believe in a soul that survives death. We call the soul or spirit, *lenapeâkàn.* When the heart stops, the soul has separated from the body and then we hold a person to be dead. At death, we believe that the spirit departs from the body but remains nearby.[53]

To prepare for a burial, a sacred red paint was applied to the face of the deceased so that the person would be recognized as Lenape when he or she stood before the Creator. Meanwhile, women of the family pounded fresh hominy from corn and baked bread for the funeral feast. Then friends, relatives, and neighbors gathered to view the body and participate in an all-night ritual. At midnight prayers began and the feast, called *takwiphâtin,* was held at the grave site. "Before everyone left," Tree Beard continues, "a small fire was made at the head of the grave, and was rekindled for the next three evenings just before sundown. This fire was made so that the deceased could take the fire with them to the spirit world to keep them warm on their journey."[54]

Tears, screaming, and wailing often accompanied a death, sometimes for weeks or even months if the deceased was an important person. In order to honor the dead, his or her name, which was considered sacred, was never spoken. Instead the deceased was referred to by his or her relationship to a living person, for example as "brother of Squanto" or "mother of Metacom."

People grieved for the dead for one entire year. Women showed they were in mourning by the way they wore their hair. If she lost her husband, a woman would wear her hair loose for a year, instead of the traditional bun worn at the back of the head by married women. The grieving wife would have no social contact for a year and would blacken her face the entire time.

After a year the widow of the deceased was smudged (purified) with cedar smoke, prayed for, and allowed to socialize again. The relatives gave her new clothes, believed to be a new skin, and she could marry again. At this time a memorial feast was held for the deceased.

Manitous, powwows, and death rituals were a continual part of the spiritual cycle of Native American life. Spiritual leadership was especially important during times of war and conflict when medicine men, shamans, and other religious leaders were called upon to guide and advise warriors and help survivors mourn for their dead.

# War and Conflict in the Northeast

Chapter 5

War and conflict between various factions of the Northeast tribes had existed for centuries before the arrival of the Europeans. As in most societies, these wars served as a means of acquiring territory, controlling trade, and gaining respect and prestige. But without written accounts, it has been difficult for historians to determine the intensity or extent of the warfare. Many Native American villages were built like fortresses to deter enemy raiders, and there was great jealousy and hatred between certain tribes.

In Massachusetts, all was peaceful when the Pilgrims arrived, but the Massachusett tribe had recently been at war with the Wampanoags and the Narragansetts, who in turn fought with each other. While the clashes between these tribes could be vicious and bloody, Native Americans rarely conducted "scorched earth" warfare in which an enemy's village was burned to the ground and all men, women, and children of a rival tribe were murdered. That was behavior learned from the invading Europeans, who fought with organized armies, powerful weapons, and ruthless efficiency.

## Native American Fighting Tactics

Native American warfare was a ritualistic enterprise much smaller in scale—and less deadly—than European warfare. Native American men were skilled warriors, and some spent their entire lives performing the rituals and rites of battle—training to fight, communicating with combat gods, planning attacks, and clashing with rival warriors. Wars could be fought over something as trivial as an insult directed at a sachem from a member of a rival tribe or something as serious as avenging the death of a loved one.

Before beginning any war, however, a sachem would send to the enemy an ambassador to recount the insults and injuries that were to be avenged. The ambassador, usually one of the ruling sachem's lieutenants, then demanded that the enemy

66

*Warriors prepare to go off to battle by participating in a war dance.*

provide an apology and material goods in order to prevent a war. If satisfaction between the parties could not be reached, war was declared, sometimes by sending the enemy a sheaf of arrows or shooting a warning arrow into a tree nearby.

Once war was declared, the entire village became involved in the preparatory ceremonies. As night fell, the warriors—who were all volunteers—gathered together. A low, steady drumbeat would begin as the war chief smeared his club with red paint, which symbolized blood. Other drummers would join in as women and children shook rattles made from gourds. Warriors began to sing and stamp the ground. Then, as DeForest writes,

those who had pledged themselves to be of the war party performed a dance. Large fires were built, and, in the lurid and fitful light of these, the warriors, fiercely painted, and grasping their arms, moved in a circle around a painted post. One of them would finally spring forward, brandish his war-club, strike furiously at the post, and go through the motions of killing and scalping it as if it were the enemy. As he performed this exercise, he vaunted the exploits he had formerly achieved, reproached the foe for cowardice, and threatened that he would kill and scalp their young men, and would lead away their women captive to his lodge.[55]

As dawn broke, the warriors ended their ceremony and the war party took to the trail, moving cautiously toward the enemy village. Warriors might be wearing a shield of two or three thicknesses of rawhide over their chest, which even the sharpest arrows could not penetrate. Then, while people of the enemy village were deep asleep in the early morning, the attackers would launch a barrage of arrows. As the defenders responded, warriors would rush in and engage them in hand-to-hand combat—there were usually no battle plans. Eventually one side or the other would prevail.

After the battle, the victors took prisoners. Sometimes the captives were adopted in place of one of the opposing tribe members

## Native American Weapons of War

Before the arrival of the Europeans, Native American warfare was conducted with bows, arrows, clubs, and tomahawks with long handles that resemble what is now called a poleax.

Clubs could simply be two- to three-foot sections of hard wood with a natural knob on one end into which a sharp point had been carved. In the hands of a strong warrior, this could easily shatter the skull of man or beast.

Native American bows were three to six feet long—the shorter bows used for hunting, the longer for war. They were made from many light, strong woods such as hickory, beech, white ash, rock maple, and witch hazel. The cord that stretched between the two ends of the bow was tough animal sinew, which was rolled tightly against the thigh of the bow maker into a long twist.

Arrow makers used strong, slender, dried alder sprouts that were two or three feet long or heart sections of white ash or cedar trees. On one end a notch was made to hold a thin, sharp piece of flint or quartz, an eagle claw, or the thin bone from a deer's shank. The back end of the arrow was decorated with the split feathers of a crow or a hawk, which helped the arrow to fly straight. All arrows bore an engraved symbol or mark of the owner so that there could be no dispute as to whose arrow brought down a duck or a deer.

Men carried up to forty or fifty arrows in a leather quiver strapped across the shoulder to permit the arrows to be grasped quickly.

who had been slain. In the family, he acted in the same position—as husband or son—as the dead man. The adopted prisoner was treated as any other member of the tribe.

On rare occasions, however, a prisoner was not adopted, and a terrible fate awaited him—a long and lingering torture that resulted in death. This torment was usually led by women, often the wife and female relatives of a slain warrior.

[The prisoner] must endure all the insults which hatred can offer, all the torments which a ferocious ingenuity can inflict, all the agonies which the human frame is able to bear. But the suffering warrior, with the flames shrivelling his skin, and the live coals scorching his flesh, sternly suppressed every sound or look which could betray his anguish, hurled back defiance in the faces of his enemies, and shouted his war-song even while the hand of death was feeling for his heartstrings.[56]

Yet by and large, Native American warfare was not especially bloody, and many battles ended in a draw. In one of the bloodiest battles between tribes ever recorded, the Uncas fought the Miantinomo in Connecticut, and only thirty men lost their lives. This tradition of relatively low casualties from war enabled the tribes to maintain balanced populations, a feature of tribal life that did not long survive the arrival of European colonists.

## A Short-Lived Peace

In 1620, the first permanent European colony in Massachusetts was founded by 102 Pilgrims on the site of a Native American village whose residents had died in the epidemics brought by European explorers in 1617–1619. The first winter in the place the Pilgrims called Plymouth was a difficult one. Starvation and disease killed half of the newcomers. No natives came forward to help them.

In 1621, however, an Abenaki from the Maine coast named Samoset, who had learned English from passing fishermen, "came bouldly amongst [the Pilgrims], and spoke to them in broken English, which they could well understand, but marvelled at."[57]

Within a few days, Samoset returned to Plymouth with a man named Tisquantum, or as the English called him, Squanto. Squanto had been kidnapped several years earlier and taken to Spain and England, where he learned to speak English. He introduced the Pilgrims to Massasoit, the head sachem of the Wampanoag who ruled over eight large villages and about thirty smaller ones. After sharing a meal, the leaders concluded a peace treaty in which the parties agreed to aid each other in case of attack. Thinking of his enemies the Narragansetts, who had not been wiped out by the plague, Massasoit welcomed the alliance with the English and their heavy artillery.

## Broken Peace in Connecticut

The Wampanoags and the Pilgrims were living under a peaceful alliance in Massachusetts. But farther south in Connecticut,

*Squanto's knowledge of the English language allowed him to help the pilgrims of Massachusetts get along with their Native neighbors.*

the powerful Pequot tribe dominated the region. The great sachem of the Pequots, Sassacus, had twenty-six sagamores under him. Together, these leaders controlled more than seven hundred warriors who presented a serious hindrance to the European colonists' expansion into the Connecticut territory.

In 1632, the Pequots were at the peak of their power after having absorbed so many tribes—and their warriors—on their long march to power. The Pequots were receiving tribute from every tribe west of the Con-

necticut River and as far north as Northfield, Massachusetts. The weaker Narragansetts refused to honor the Pequots' power, and a permanent state of war existed between the two tribes.

The Pequots did not approve of their new Pilgrim neighbors to the north and became angry when Dutch fur traders began to establish forts in the Connecticut region. Soon the Dutch were joined in Connecticut by English settlers from Massachusetts. And when the English held the first meeting of the General Court of Connecticut in the 1630s, they decided, "there shalbe an offensive warr agt [against] the Pequoitt."[58]

By blaming the Pequots for the murders of several traders in 1634 and 1635 (murders, in fact, committed by other tribes), the English created an excuse to launch an attack on Connecticut's most powerful tribe. After several skirmishes in which Native Americans were murdered and their villages, canoes, and fields destroyed, the English prepared for their final assault.

## Armed Assaults Against the Natives

In early June 1637, three hundred armed Englishmen from Connecticut and Massachusetts marched to the main Pequot village on the Mystic River. The village was protected by palisades, was about one acre

## Squanto and the First Thanksgiving

In 1614 an English sea captain named Thomas Hunt kidnapped twenty-four Native Americans in Massachusetts and sold them as slaves in Malaga, Spain. Several of the victims were ransomed by monks, including a member of the Patuxet tribe named Tisquantum, or Squanto. After three years working for the monks, Squanto escaped and made his way to England, where he was befriended by a wealthy merchant who taught him to speak English. In 1619, Squanto made his way back across the ocean to Massachusetts only to find his entire village deserted and his relatives and friends dead from European diseases.

In 1620, when the Pilgrims landed at Plymouth, they were shocked when Squanto walked into their village and spoke to them in English. Squanto, who understood the power and wealth of the colonists after having seen Europe, introduced the Pilgrims to a Wampanoag grand sachem who signed a peace treaty with the English. Later, Squanto began to help the Pilgrims. William Bradford wrote in *History of the Plymouth Plantation,*

"[Squanto] directed them how to set their corne, wher to take fish, and to procure other comodities, and was also their pilott to bring them to unknowne places for their profitt, and never left them till he dyed."

When Squanto explained the traditional Native American harvesttime festival to the English, the Pilgrims decided to have the first Thanksgiving with ninety members of the Wampanoag, who brought five deer for the communal feast. For three days, the Pilgrims and natives prayed, sang, and held sporting contests. The English and Wampanoag promised to make the feast an annual celebration, and the two factions remained at peace for forty years.

in size, and contained seventy wigwams. The night before the attack, the English soldiers secretly surrounded the village. They were joined by nearly three hundred Mohegan and Narragansett warriors. (The Pequots were once part of the Mohegans but had split from the tribe around 1590, and the two tribes had since become bitter enemies.)

The Native American sentries reported that the Pequots did not suspect an attack and, as Captain John Mason wrote, the sentries

heard the Enemy [Pequot] Singing at the *Fort,* who continued that Strain until Midnight, with great Insulting and Rejoicing. . . . They . . . concluded we

*Soldiers destroy a small Pequot fort by burning houses and killing their inhabitants.*

were affraid of them and durst not come near them: the Burthen of their Song tending to that purpose.[59]

The attack at dawn completely surprised the Pequots, who were sleeping in their wigwams. The attackers first set the straw roofs of the wigwams on fire, and with the aid of a strong wind, the large village was quickly consumed by flames. As men, women, and children fled the inferno, they were shot by waiting soldiers. Others ran back to certain death inside their burning homes.

And indeed such a dreadful Terror did the ALMIGHTY let fall upon

their Spirits, that they would fly from us and run into the very Flames, where many of them perished. And when the *Fort* was thoroughly Fired, Command was given, that all should fall off and surround the *Fort.* . . .

The Fire was [rekindled] on the *North East Side* to windward; which did swiftly over run the *Fort,* to the extream Amazement of the Enemy, and great Rejoycing of ourselves.[60]

Out of the four hundred Pequots who lived within the village palisades, only five people survived. The Massachusetts General Court set aside June 14 as a Day of

Thanksgiving for the victory. In Connecticut, Captain John Mason was given five hundred acres of land that had belonged to the Pequot, with another five hundred acres to be divided between his troops.

## Extermination of the Pequots

Seven hundred Pequots lived outside the razed village, and these remaining people were hunted down like animals. They fled westward toward Dutch-held lands, but slowed by the old and the very young, they were tracked to a swamp near Quinnipiac. As night fell, the pursuers surrounded the trapped Native Americans. The circle closed in the morning and the English, Narragansett, and Mohegan warriors saw

> Heaps of them sitting close together, upon whom they discharged their Peices laden with ten or twelve Pistol-bullets at a Time, putting the Muzles of their Peices under the Boughs within a few yeards of them; so as besides those that were found Dead . . . it was judged that many more were killed and sunk into the Mire, and never were minded more by Friend or Fo.[61]

Several dozen Pequots remained. Some fled to Mohawk territory in the west,

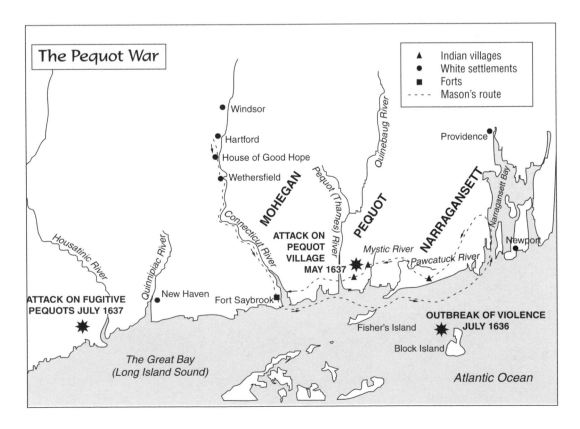

The Pequot War

Indian villages
White settlements
Forts
- - - - Mason's route

Windsor

Hartford

House of Good Hope

Wethersfield

Providence

MOHEGAN

PEQUOT

NARRAGANSETT

Quinebaug River

Pequot (Thames) River

Narragansett Bay

Connecticut River

Quinnipiac River

Housatinic River

ATTACK ON PEQUOT VILLAGE MAY 1637

Mystic River

Pawcatuck River

Newport

ATTACK ON FUGITIVE PEQUOTS JULY 1637

New Haven    Fort Saybrook

Fisher's Island

OUTBREAK OF VIOLENCE JULY 1636

Block Island

The Great Bay (Long Island Sound)

Atlantic Ocean

where they were killed by that tribe. Several hundred were taken as vassals by the Mohegans and Narragansetts. Others were sold into slavery and became the first slaves to colonists in New England.

Within two years of the overthrow of the Pequots, the foundations were laid for the towns of Guilford, Milford, Stratford, Fairfield, Norwalk, and Stamford, where Pequot villages had existed for thousands of years.

The destruction of the tribe also changed the balance of power in New England. Every tribe was now forced to ac-

knowledge the power and the authority of the colonial governments. As one official stated, "The Overthrow given the Pequots struck such a Terror into all the *Indians* in those Parts . . . that they sought our Friendship, and tendered to be under our Protection."[62]

## Conflicts over Trade Goods and Alcohol

In the decades following the Pequot War, the daily lives of the surviving tribes in the Northeast became closely linked with those of the Europeans. The colonists in-

*Native Americans crowd into a general store to purchase European goods. The Indians used many European tools because they were superior to their own.*

troduced the tribes to a wide array of manufactured goods including metals, cooking utensils, cloth, glass beads, steel knives, muskets, and alcoholic beverages. Native Americans who acquired these goods also gained prestige and power.

There were many downsides to the flood of new European trade goods. When the Native Americans first encountered the items, they were amazed at how much easier they made daily life. Within twenty or thirty years, however, these goods, especially those made of metal, had become necessities and encouraged a fundamental change of lifestyle.

When items such as iron pots, knives, and weapons became accepted into the native culture, people began to lose the skills needed to make these items with traditional methods and materials. Within a generation, few among the natives remembered how to manufacture items necessary for daily life from wood or stone. Because of their dependence on European goods, the tribes were soon forced to turn to the fur trade to sustain them. Due to heavy trapping, however, many furbearing animals became harder to find in New England. This drove tribes into hunting grounds claimed by other tribes, increasing competition and hostility.

The traders also brought alcohol to the Native Americans, who at first believed that it was a magical potion that could inspire dreams, a much-sought-after experience. Next to smallpox and other epidemics, alcohol proved by far the most destructive force to the Native Americans.

Before the arrival of the Europeans, a majority of Native American tribes had had absolutely no exposure to alcohol. Thus, as liquor came into common use in villages, the rum, brandy, beer, and wine had a destructive effect and caused a host of problems that Native Americans had never faced before. Drunken men quarreled with their wives and neighbors. Conflicts sometimes ended in violence. Traders often plied Indians with alcohol in order to take advantage of them in trades, sometimes acquiring a season's worth of pelts for two or three bottles of rum.

## King Philip Challenges the Puritans

As the number of European settlers increased and their society began to dominate the lives of the Wampanoag in Massachusetts, the peace established with the Pilgrims was becoming more difficult to maintain. Historian Alvin M. Josephy Jr. paints a grim picture:

By 1662, some forty thousand English colonists lived in New England, about twice the size of the Indian population. Wherever the English were most densely settled, the Indians were precariously surrounded and outnumbered, their shrunken and depleted hunting lands allowing them little choice for livelihood but to work for the English as laborers and servants alongside slaves. Zealous Puritan authorities, with no

## King Philip's Grievances

King Philip had many grievances concerning the British. These were written down by Rhode Island governor John Easton in *Diary of King Philip's War 1675–1676.* (Easton refers to Philip and other Native American men as kings, and native women as queens.)

"[The Indians] said, they had been the first in doing good to the English, and the English the first in doing wrong; when the English first came, the king's father was as a great man, and the English as a little child; he constrained other Indians from wronging the English, and gave them corn and showed them how to plant, and was free to do them any good, and had let them have a hundred times more land than now the king had for his own people. . . .

And another grievance was, if twenty of their honest Indians testified that an Englishman had done them wrong, it was as nothing; and if but one of their worst Indians testified against any Indian or their king, when it pleased the English, it was sufficient.

Another grievance was, when their kings sold land, the English would say it was more than they agreed to, and a writing must be proof against all of them; and some of their kings had done wrong to sell so much that they left their people none; and some being given to drunkenness the English made them drunk and then cheated them in bargains. Now their kings were forewarned not to part with land for nothing, in comparison to the value thereof. . . .

Another grievance, the English were so eager to sell the Indians liquors that most of the Indians spent all in drunkenness and then ravened upon the sober Indians and they did believe often did hurt English cattle, and their kings could not prevent it."

regard for the laws or customs of sovereign Indian nations, vigorously prosecuted Indians for hunting and fishing on the Sabbath, using Indian medicines, or entering into non-Christian marital unions. In Plymouth itself, where Massasoit's people and the struggling Pilgrims had once joined to give thanks in their own ways, Indians now faced a sentence of death for denying the Christian religion.[63]

At that time, the sachem of the Wampanoags was named Metacom, but he was known to the colonists as King Philip. The son of Massasoit, Philip was a tall, slim warrior who was known for his skillful oratory. With a quick, agile mind and the ability to mesmerize his followers with his fiery speeches denouncing English attacks on Native American property, culture, religion, and values, Philip represented a serious threat to white authorities.

Philip realized that his tribe would never be free unless the English were driven from the shores of North America. For more than four years, he planned relentlessly for war. While the older tribe members were unwilling to engage the English in what promised to be a long, hard series of battles, hundreds of young warriors were ready to fight.

## King Philip's War

In 1674, a Christianized Native American named John Sassamon began to spy on the Wampanoags. In December, he told the Puritans that Philip was planning to attack

*A European trades alcohol with a Native American. Alcohol was unknown to Native Americans before the European arrival and Indians proved especially vulnerable to its harmful effects.*

the white settlement of Swansea. A month later, Sassamon was found with a broken neck near his home. Although the Puritans had no proof of who killed Sassamon, they hanged three Wampanoag subsachems, including one man who was Philip's closest adviser.

Enraged that the English had interfered in Native American affairs, Philip spoke out so fiercely that his followers initiated a two-week-long war dance. On June 20, 1675, a group of young Wampanoag warriors invaded Swansea while the settlers were in church. Word of the attack spread quickly, and the next day war erupted.

In a series of attacks, Native Americans ransacked and burned the Massachusetts communities of Rehoboth, Taunton, Dartmouth, and Middleborough. William Hubbard described one of the attacks:

> [On] March 28 they burnt thirty Barns, and near upon forty dwelling Houses, thereby as it were threatening the utter Desolation of that poor Town; and so proceeding on that Side of the Country, they burnt the very next Day about thirty Houses in *Providence* in the Way toward *Narhaganset.*[64]

As the panic of the settlers intensified, they unwittingly aided Philip's cause by attacking any and all Native Americans in the area—even those sympathetic to the British. Troops burned villages and supplies of friendly Pocumtuks, Nonatooks, Squakheags, and Nashaways—all tribes that had long lived in peace with colonists.

These tribes rose in vengeance and joined with Philip's warriors.

As 1675 drew to a close, colonial soldiers assaulted a Narragansett village on a snowy December day. Although the Narragansetts sided with the British, the soldiers set fire to five hundred dwellings in the village, and the flames were whipped to a fury by the icy north wind. More than six hundred men, women, and children were "terribly Barbikew'd"[65] according to Puritan cleric Cotton Mather.

## The Tide Turns Against Philip

Philip's warriors launched a new series of attacks in February 1676, burning every building and killing every colonist they encountered. On February 9, they burned the town of Lancaster, killing fifty people. On the 20th, they assaulted Medfield, less than twenty miles from Boston. In May, Philip's warriors daringly burned sixteen homesteads within five miles of Plymouth. By the end of spring, the grand sachem's men had struck fifty-two of the ninety settlements in the region, destroying twelve, heavily damaging many others, and killing more than six hundred colonists. Victory for the Native Americans seemed at hand.

Philip's warriors were not used to sustaining long-term warfare, however, and as summer approached, many left to plow their gardens and feed their families. Others decided they could not beat the powerful English who, it was said, had resolved to eradicate the Natives Americans once and for all by putting more soldiers into the field.

*Native Americans and colonists brutally attack each other during King Philip's War. King Philip was able to rally his Indian allies to form one of the most capable armies ever formed by Native Americans.*

Some of Philip's closest allies decided to make peace with the colonists. By summer, the grand sachem's men were starving. The English militia was rounding them up one by one, selling them into slavery, hanging them, or putting them before firing squads. The English also continued to destroy dozens of Native American villages.

In August of 1676, the English militia fell upon Philip's last remaining warriors, killing or capturing 173. Philip's wife and nine-year-old son were taken as prisoners and sold into slavery to planters in the West Indies for a few English pounds. "My heart breaks," Philip reportedly cried out after the battle; "now I am ready to die."[66]

Philip returned to the camp where his father Massasoit had once fed and entertained the Pilgrims. At dawn on August 12, 1676, the English army surrounded Philip's camp, and within minutes the grand sachem lay dead, killed by a musket ball through the heart. His head was cut off and displayed on a pole in Plymouth for the next twenty years.

King Philip's war was the bloodiest ever fought in New England. Six hundred English were killed, twelve hundred homes were burned, and eight thousand cattle were slain. The Wampanoag, Nipmuc, and

Narragansett nations lost three thousand people. Only one hundred Narragansetts and two hundred Wampanoags survived. Many smaller tribes became virtually extinct. As Colin G. Calloway writes,

> The war dragged on in the north and pulled in the Abenakis from Maine, but the outcome was sealed. . . . [T]he killing of [King Philip] came to symbolize an end to Indian independence, the last gasp of a way of life already battered and broken.[67]

The Native American population in New England that only one hundred years earlier numbered seventy thousand souls was practically extinct.

# Chapter 6

# From King Philip to the Twenty-First Century

New England Native American history often stops with the killing of King Philip and the destruction of the Wampanoags. But the descendants of the former rulers of the entire East Coast still remain within New England society. After the war, most of the tribes were confined to small reservations, their lands confiscated. In Massachusetts and Connecticut, European guardians were appointed to protect Native American lands and resources that remained. But the guardians were often corrupt and sold lands they were appointed to safeguard.

Some natives abandoned their tribal heritage, converted to Christianity, and attended schools run by missionaries. Others, who owed money to colonists, were forced to work as servants in their homes. William Apess, a Pequot author of several books, wrote in 1835 about the plight of the Marshpee (or Mashpee) tribe in Massachusetts:

> [The] Marshpee Indians were enslaved by the laws of Massachusetts, and deprived of every civil right which belongs to man. White Overseers had power to tear their children from them and bind them out where they pleased. They could also sell the services of any adult Indian on the Plantation they chose to call idle, for three years at a time, and send him where they pleased, renewing the lease every three years, and thus, make him a slave for life.[68]

Census figures from the eighteenth century shed light on the numbers of Native Americans surviving in New England. In South Kingston, Rhode Island, in 1730, for instance, there were 935 British colonists, 333 African Americans (free and slave), and 223 Native American slaves. Another census estimated that 33.5 percent of all Native Americans in Rhode Island were living with white families in 1774.

## Land Rights Ceded

After King Philip's War, the governments of the English colonies used all of their

*European colonists and Native Americans gather to work on a peace treaty. Often these peace treaties resulted in Indians giving up much of their ancestral lands to colonists.*

powers to acquire tribal land. In some cases money changed hands, but often colonial authorities simply cut down forests and built settlements on land that had belonged to Native Americans. As their hunting and agricultural lands disappeared, the Native Americans were forced into poverty and starvation, which often motivated them to sell their remaining lands so they could buy food and supplies.

The Indian Trade and Intercourse Act of 1790 specifically prohibited the transfer of Indian lands without congressional ap-proval, but well into the nineteenth century, Massachusetts and Maine continued to make treaties that confiscated huge tracts of Native American territory.

In Maine's Penobscot Valley, the Penobscots signed away almost two hundred thousand acres in the late eighteenth century. By 1818, they had given up all of their remaining land except the islands in the Penobscot River and four six-mile-square townships. In 1833, the state of Maine paid fifty thousand dollars for the four townships. By the mid–nineteenth century, the Penobscots were confined to one community on Indian Island at Old Town, and the Passamaquoddies were reduced to two reservations at Pleasant Point and Peter Dana Point.

In *After King Philip's War,* Colin G. Calloway writes about the attitudes of white New Englanders toward their Native American neighbors:

> Stephen Badger, minister at the Indian town of Natick, Massachusetts, reported in 1798 that Indians were "generally considered by white people, and placed, as if by common consent, in an inferiour and degraded situation, and treated accordingly." Covetous white neighbors "took every advantage of them that they could, under colour of legal authority . . . to dishearten and depress them." At Stockbridge, Indians were surrounded by "Designing People who aim at Geting Away all that The Indians are Possessed of." Traders would sell Indian people liquor, encourage them to run up debts, then take them to court for nonpayment of the debts. Indians would be compelled to sell their lands "at a very low rate, in order to have their debts discharged." Such schemes left them "impoverished and disheartened."[69]

Diseases and epidemics also took their toll, killing half the Native Americans on Nantucket between 1600 and 1670. By 1770, that population had been reduced by 90 percent.

In 1880, the Rhode Island state legislature declared the Narragansett tribe extinct, revoked their tribal status, and sold their land at public auction except for a two-acre plot that contained a church and cemetery.

## Scattered to the Winds and Seas

After King Philip's War, the remaining Wampanoag migrated north and west. Many tribe members joined the Abenaki in Maine, Vermont, and New Hampshire, but in the eighteenth century their relatives were forced to move even farther north, into Quebec. In the 1780s, the Narragansetts who remained in Rhode Island sold off the rest of their lands and joined other tribes. Native Americans from other tribes in the region had their lands reduced to such a small area that they no longer could support themselves. They migrated to Brotherton, New York, to start a small community there. Around 1790, Spanish explorers in the American heartland met members of Maine's Abenaki tribe who were living as far west as Arkansas and Missouri.

> Indian people who had once moved seasonally for subsistence purposes were now compelled to move about by poverty and the search for work or dislocated relatives. White observers concluded that Indians were "addicted to wander from place to place" and "naturally inclined to a roving and unsettled life." Ministers

# Working the Whaling Ships

At the end of the seventeenth century, whale oil and whale bone were valuable commodities. A full-grown adult whale could yield up to 120 barrels of oil— enough to keep thousands of lanterns in Boston and New York burning night after night. This was in addition to 750 pounds of bone that was used for everything from tools to buttons. Hundreds of the gigantic animals could be seen swimming off the coast of Nantucket Island, once home to twenty-five hundred members of the Wampanoag and Nauset tribes.

The availability of cheap land for farming in New England caused a serious labor shortage for industries such as whaling, which was dangerous and difficult work. Colin G. Calloway's edited volume *After King Philip's War* contains a description by Paul Dudley, a seventeenth-century whaling expert, of how whales were hunted: "The Whale is sometimes killed with a single Stroke, and yet at other Times she will hold the Whale-men in Play, near half a Day together."

Because of their skill as whale-men and their availability as laborers, Nantucket's first commercial whalers were Native Americans. This often took the men to sea for two or three years at a time, separating them from their wives and children. In addition, the Englishmen who owned the whaling ships charged the Na-

tive American workers inflated prices for all of their food, clothing, liquor, and other supplies while they were working on board. By the time the workers returned home several years later, the money that they were supposed to have made was kept by the ship owners as payment for supplies. In spite of this, in 1830, one man wrote: "Nearly every boat was manned in part, many almost entirely, by natives: some of the most active of them were made steersmen, and some were allowed even to head the boats."

*Indian whalers work in the waters of New England. Although difficult and dangerous work, whaling had many rewards because it became such a prosperous trade.*

*Indians create a camp along the St. Lawrence River. After King Philip's War, it was hard for Indians of New England to keep or obtain any land.*

worried that such a "wandering and irregular practice" threatened the morals and health of Indian women and children, but New England towns often "warned out" [expelled] needy people to avoid paying poor relief [welfare costs] thereby adding to the numbers of Indian people traveling the roads.[70]

Because the males were so often away from home seeking employment, many Native American women married Portuguese, German, African American, and other men. Such intermingling made it difficult for Native Americans to maintain their cultural heritage in many instances and harder for them to claim their tribal rights.

The prevailing view from the nineteenth century portrayed Native Americans as fading from sight, having become a doomed race. As Colin G. Calloway observed,

Nowhere did Indian extinction seem more assured than in New England. John Adams, writing to Thomas Jefferson in 1812, recalled growing up seventy years earlier with Indians for neighbors and as visitors to his father's house. A large Indian family had lived in the town, and Adams nostalgically remembered visiting their wigwam and being treated with blackberries, strawberries, whortle berries, apples, plums, and peaches. "But the Girls went out to Service and the Boys to Sea, till not a Soul is left," he wrote. "We scarcely see an Indian in a year." In his Report on Indian Affairs, submitted to the secretary of war in 1822, Jedidiah Morse portrayed the Indian communities in New England as a "few feeble remnants" teetering on the brink of extinction. "All the Indian tribes who once inhabited the territory of New England—the Narragansetts, the Mohicans, the Pequots—now live only in men's memories," wrote [French observer] Alexis de Tocqueville in 1833 after his visit to the United States.[71]

Native Americans never disappeared completely from New England. Because of continued racism, however, generations of Native Americans found life was easier if they did not draw attention to themselves and did not reveal their ancestry. In spite of their loss of land, language, and culture, many Native Americans retained their "Indianness" through faith, family, and community.

It was not until the early twentieth century, however, that Native Americans began to show their cultural identity again at fairs, public events, and other ceremonies. Native people in New England brought together regional networks to study and honor their past traditions. The New England Indian Council was one such network that formed in 1923, adopting the motto "I still live."

# Changing Policies of Government

Although Native Americans at times have been guaranteed rights to various tracts of land by state and federal governments, these land rights were modified to fit political whims and fashion. Rarely before the 1980s did these changes benefit the tribes. For example, a series of federal laws to regulate trade and other dealings between whites and the tribes has been on the books since George Washington's first term in office. Section 1 of the Trade and Intercourse Act made it illegal to trade with tribes without a license. Section 4 of the act outlawed sales of Native American land to individuals or states without the written permission of the U.S. government. However, the federal government was weak at that time and was not able to keep the states from making their own deals with the tribes.

In 1794, the Passamaquoddy ceded 1 million acres to the state of Massachusetts. The treaty was never legal and would later be declared invalid, but having given up a huge portion of their lands, the tribe was forced to move to the Pleasant Point Reservation in Maine. In 1796, the Penobscot yielded two hundred thousand acres of land in return for an annual supply of 150 yards of blue cloth, 400 pounds of shot, 100 pounds of gunpowder, 100 bushels of corn, and a barrel of rum. With nowhere to hunt, the tribe had little use for the gunpowder.

# Fighting for the White Armies

When the colonists threw off the yoke of English rule in the Revolutionary War, Native Americans fought for the cause of liberty, often with terrible consequences. In the book *On Our Own Ground,* William Apess wrote in 1835 about soldiers in the Revolution who came from Mashpee.

"The whole regiment, drawn from the whole County of Barnstable, mustered but 149 men, nearly *one-fifth* of whom were volunteers from the little Indian Plantation of Marshpee, which then did not contain over one hundred male heads of families! No white town in the County furnished anything like this proportion of the 149 volunteers. The Indian soldiers fought through the war; and as far as we have been able to ascertain the fact, from documents or tradition, all but one, fell martyrs to liberty, in the struggle for Independence. There is but one Indian now living, who receives the reward of his services as a revolutionary soldier, old Isaac Wickham. . . . Parson Holly, in a memorial to the Legislature in 1783, states that most of the women in Marshpee, had lost their husbands in the war. At that time there were seventy widows on the Plantation."

Native Americans from the Northeast also fought in the War of 1812 and the Civil War. Men from New England tribes served with honor in all of America's wars in the twentieth century, including World Wars I and II, Korea, and Vietnam.

*Ironically, Indians fought alongside colonists against English rule in the Revolutionary War.*

In 1820, when Maine became a state (it had been part of Massachusetts until that time) the Abenaki claimed only a few thousand acres out of the huge territory that had been their homeland. Even this was taken from them by the state, which ignored the restrictions of the 1790 law and sold off their lands piecemeal for the

## The Real Cleveland Indian

In modern times, Native Americans have protested against sports teams that use Indian names for their teams or mascots. Team names like the Braves and the Redskins are considered racial slurs by Native Americans. But one team, the Cleveland Indians, was actually named to honor Louis Francis Sockalexis, a member of the Penobscot tribe from Old Town, Maine.

Sockalexis played baseball at Holy Cross College and Notre Dame in 1897 and was later drafted to play outfield for the Cleveland Spiders. Sockalexis batted .338 and stole sixteen bases his first year on the field. A drinking problem cut short the career of the Penobscot ballplayer, and he quit the league in 1899. As an honor to his athletic feats, the Cleveland Spiders franchise changed its name to the Cleveland Indians. Sockalexis died in 1913 at the age of forty-two.

rest of the century. The remaining tribe members were forced to live on welfare and charity, giving the government even more control over their lives. Their children attended schools where they were punished for speaking their native language. Young people left the reservations in increasing numbers, and traditions were forgotten as old people died.

The federal government granted Native Americans full citizenship in 1924 and gave them voting rights for the first time. But the state of Maine would not allow its original inhabitants to vote until 1954.

In 1953, federal policy changed once again. The government wanted to get "out of the Indian business," and to that end an act of Congress instituted a policy known as "termination" and named dozens of tribes whose land-trust status would be terminated as soon as possible. This law allowed the government to revoke the special status that protected Indian reservations and to transfer federal responsibility to state governments. Another part of this policy was to encourage Native Americans to move to big cities.

Between 1954 and 1962 Congress passed a series of laws terminating the federal recognition of more than one hundred tribes. The stated purpose of these laws was to integrate Native Americans into American society. Despite such lofty words, 133 separate bills to transfer Native American land claims to non-Indians were introduced in Congress. In the mid-1960s, the federal government began to reject the tribal termination concept.

*Native Americans line up to register to vote.*

## Victory at Last for the First Americans

In 1980, the tribes saw the first in a new wave of victories. In 1970, the Passamaquoddy and Penobscot took the government to court, claiming that in selling the tribal lands, the state of Maine had violated the Trade and Intercourse Act of 1790. After a ten-year court battle, President Jimmy Carter signed the Maine Indians Claims Settlement Act awarding $81.5 million to the tribes in compensation for property taken from them over the centuries.

These dramatic changes established precedents that benefited other native peoples. In 1979, the Narragansetts were awarded the return of eighteen hundred acres of tribal land and secured federal recognition as an Indian tribe. Recognition is important because it grants tribes certain rights and benefits, including health services and education, financing for building reservations and housing, and funds for new land for tribal expansion.

In 1983, descendants of the powerful seventeenth-century Pequots won federal recognition, and the tribe, which had been thought extinct, soon became a major economic force in southern New England. The Pequots opened a gaming casino, founded a tribal museum, and sponsored archaeological projects and historic conferences. The casino, the world's largest, has generated hundreds of millions of dollars, making the Mashantucket Pequot Tribal Nation the wealthiest tribe in the United States. The Pequots also own Pequot River Shipworks, Fox Navigation, the Pequot Pharmaceutical Network, and three Connecticut hotels.

The official website of the Mashantucket Pequot Museum and Research Center summarizes recent developments:

With the assistance of the Native American Rights Fund and the Indian Rights Association, the Tribe filed suit in 1976 against neighboring landowners to recover land that had been sold by the State of Connecticut in 1856. Seven years later the Pequots reached a settlement with the landowners, who agreed that the 1856 sale was illegal. . . . The state responded, and the Connecticut Legislature unanimously passed legislation to petition the federal government to grant tribal recognition to the Mashantucket Pequots and settle the claim. With help from the Connecticut delegation, the Mashantucket Pequot Indian Land Claims Settlement Act was enacted by

the U.S. Congress and signed by President Reagan on Oct. 18, 1983. . . . Currently, the reservation is 1,250 acres. . . .

In 1986, the Tribe opened its bingo operation, followed, in 1992, by the establishment of the first phase of Foxwoods Resort Casino. The . . . Mashantucket Pequot Museum and Research Center [opened on August 11, 1998] is located on the Mashantucket Pequot Reservation, where many members of the Mashantucket Pequot tribal members continue to live. It is one of the oldest, continuously occupied Indian reservations in North America.[72]

Former enemies of the Pequots have also come into their own. The Mohegan Nation obtained federal recognition in 1994, after a sixteen-year process that entailed the review of twenty thousand pages of paperwork. Although the tribe's sovereignty had been recognized continuously by Connecticut from colonial times to the present, corrupt practices by state officials had forced the Mohegan leadership to disband the original reservation. Some of this territory was reacquired by the tribe and placed in trust by the U.S. government. In 1995 the Mohegans opened a casino.

## Wampanoag Survival
After King Philip's War, only four hundred Wampanoag remained alive, mostly on the island of Martha's Vineyard. The

*Mashantucket Pequot Museum and Research Center is a reminder of Native American life in North America. Native Americans continue to petition the United States government for money and land grants as payment for what the tribes lost in previous centuries.*

Nantucket branch of the Wampanoags survived in their island community and reached about seven hundred people until a fever epidemic in 1763 killed two-thirds of the Nantuckets. The last surviving member of that band died in 1855. The Martha's Vineyard community survived by adding members of other tribes. By 1807, however, there were only forty full-blooded Wampanoags alive.

The Commonwealth of Massachusetts divided the tribal lands in 1842 and ended the tribal status of the Wampanoags in 1870, but the tribe re-formed as the Wampanoag Nation in 1928 and today has about three thousand members. There are five bands of Wampanoag in Massachusetts at Assonet, Gay Head, Herring Pond, Mashpee, and Namasket. All have tried to gain federal and state recognition, but only six hundred Gay Head members were successful in 1987. A request by twenty-two hundred members of the Mashpee was turned down by the federal courts in 1978.

This has not stopped the Wampanoag from asserting their rights. Tribal members

## Native American Casinos

The federal Indian Gaming Regulatory Act (IGRA) of 1988 allows Native Americans to operate gambling, or gaming, casinos on reservation land. To take advantage of this opportunity, Native Americans immediately began construction of Las Vegas–style gambling casinos. Casinos located near larger cities and towns became very popular and generated huge revenues for tribes.

As of February, 1997, 115 tribes had gambling operations in twenty-four states, several of them in New England. One of the more popular casinos was the Pequot tribe's Foxwoods Resort Casino in Ledyard, Connecticut, which employs more than eleven thousand people and in 1998 made an estimated $1 billion.

Although some believe Indian gaming has made average Native Americans rich, tribes are utilizing most the profits to pay off costs incurred to go into gaming, such as building casinos, hotels, restaurants, and roads. The rest of the money is going toward building self-sufficiency and government infrastructure on reservations. Since IGRA allows only the tribal governments (not individuals) to enter into gaming, the tribes are using their gaming profits for law enforcement, education, economic development, tribal courts, and infrastructure improvement such as building new houses, schools, roads, and sewer and water systems. This money also benefits individuals by funding social service programs, scholarships, health care clinics, chemical dependency treatment programs, and other uses.

But casinos have benefited only a small number of tribes in the Northeast. The rest are working with little assistance to break a centuries-old cycle of poverty.

have a strong lobbying presence in state and federal government and continue to press for land rights, education and health benefits, and federal recognition.

Like other New England tribes, the Wampanoag still come together to hold religious ceremonies, which include unity circles and powwows. When a unity circle is held, neighbors and families gather to dance, sing, drum, and feast on traditional foods. At the close of the ceremony, the ashes from the fire are preserved and reused at the next unity circle. This symbolizes the belief that the Native Americans' fire will never be extinguished.

The most important powwow for the Wampanoags is held in Mashpee during the July Fourth weekend. The powwow lasts three days and draws Native Americans and tourists from all across New England. The powwow begins with a grand sachem and medicine man leading tribal officers and dancers into a circle where drummers are playing. The outdoor arena pulsates with the beat of the drums and the bells ringing on the feet of the dancers. The performers wear ceremonial clothing that is a combination of traditional Wampanoag deerskin and Plains Indian attire. The grand sachem welcomes the crowd and gives a prayer to the spirits.

After the ceremony, crowds gather to buy traditional foods such as steamed quahogs, clam cakes, boiled lobster, and corn on the cob. Artwork and crafts such as jewelry, clothing, beads, pottery, and baskets may be purchased.

## New England Natives in the Twenty-First Century

The native tribes of New England were considered a "doomed race" at the beginning of the twentieth century, but enormous changes have occurred. The population of the tribes has increased dramatically, along with their power. Although more than three centuries of poverty, unemployment, and discrimination have taken their toll, many Indian nations are reasserting their strength, pride, and traditional culture.

The success of the Puritan colonists—and the country that was founded in their wake—owes a great debt to the Native Americans of the Northeast. It was from the original Native American gifts to them—corn, beans, and squash—that the Puritans were able to survive and thrive.

There is much else for which modern New England is indebted to the Indians. Travel in any direction . . . and you will follow the winding ways and easy grades originally worn deep by moccasined feet. The very names of a number of principle highways—"Bay Path," "Ossipee Trail," "Mohawk Trail," "Old Connecticut Path,"—bespeak their origin. The hills, rivers, ponds, and mountains that these roads skirt have the musical titles the original inhabitants gave them: Winnepesaukee, Quinsigamond, Quinnipiack, Narragansett, Monadnock, Connecticut, Kennebec, Katahdin, Merrimac, Wachusett. Flourishing cities and charming towns are seated on the spots that in the distant past vanished tribes selected as the most suitable for habitation.[73]

The first people of New England have contributed more than just foods and place names: Native Americans have given the United States an important part of its cultural heritage.

So when Native Americans gather at unity ceremonies and powwows, the talk is not of shattered dreams or broken treaties but of hope for the future, of the medicine hoop mended and connected again, of the resources the first Americans have today to help them remain spiritually strong and culturally relevant. For these are people who—in the face of every disaster and calamity that can befall a people—have survived.

# Notes

## Introduction: The First Americans

1. Quoted in Alvin M. Josephy Jr., *500 Nations*. New York: Alfred A. Knopf, 1994, p. 214.
2. Francis Jennings, *The Invasion of America*. Chapel Hill: University of North Carolina Press, 1975, p. 15.
3. David Horowitz, *The First Frontier: The Indian Wars & America's Origins: 1607–1776*. New York: Simon & Schuster, 1978, p. 17.
4. Jennings, *The Invasion of America*, p. 59.

## Chapter 1: Native Peoples of the Northeast

5. William A. Haviland and Marjory W. Power, *The Original Vermonters*. Hanover, NH: University Press of New England, 1981, pp. 151–52.
6. Quoted in William S. Simmons, *Spirit of the New England Tribes*. Hanover, NH: University Press of New England, 1986, p. 15.
7. Samuel de Champlain, *Voyages of Samuel de Champlain 1604–1618*. 1907. Reprint, New York: Barnes & Noble, 1946, p. 95.
8. Lee Sultzman, "Nauset History," Geographic Overview of First Nations Histories (no date given). www.dickshovel.com/up.html.

9. John W. DeForest, *History of the Indians of Connecticut*. 1851. Reprint, New Haven, CT: Archon Books, 1964, p. 61.
10. Sultzman, "Mahican History," Geographic Overview of First Nations Histories (no date given). www.dickshovel.com/up.html.
11. Clinton Alfred Weslager, *The Delaware Indians*. New Brunswick, NJ: Rutgers University Press, 1972, pp. 32–33.
12. Howard S. Russell, *Indian New England Before the Mayflower*. Hanover, NH: University Press of New England, 1980, pp. 23–24.
13. Russell, *Indian New England Before the Mayflower*, pp. 27–28.

## Chapter 2: Villages of the Northeast Tribes

14. DeForest, *History of the Indians of Connecticut*, p. 2.
15. DeForest, *History of the Indians of Connecticut*, p. 15.
16. Quoted in Herbert Milton Sylvester, *Indian Wars of New England*, vol. 1. Boston: W. B. Clarke Company, 1910, pp. 103–104.
17. DeForest, *History of the Indians of Connecticut*, p. 12.
18. Champlain, *Voyages of Samuel de Champlain 1604–1618*, pp. 313–14.

19. Russell, *Indian New England Before the Mayflower,* p. 56.

20. Josephy, *500 Nations,* p. 208.

21. Hitakonanu'laxk, *The Grandfathers Speak.* New York: Interlink Books, 1994, pp. 15–16.

22. Quoted in Russell, *Indian New England Before the Mayflower,* p. 96.

23. Russell, *Indian New England Before the Mayflower,* p. 96.

24. Weslager, *The Delaware Indians*, p. 62.

25. Quoted in W. P. Cumming, S. E. Hillier, D. B. Quinn, and G. Williams, *The Exploration of North America 1630–1776.* New York: G. P. Putnam's Sons, 1974, pp. 75–76.

26. Russell, *Indian New England Before the Mayflower,* p. 20.

**Chapter 3: The Seasons of Life**

27. DeForest, *History of the Indians of Connecticut,* p. 3.

28. Quoted in Russell, *Indian New England Before the Mayflower,* p. 166.

29. DeForest, *History of the Indians of Connecticut,* pp. 8–9.

30. Quoted in Russell, *Indian New England Before the Mayflower*, p. 125.

31. Champlain, *Voyages of Samuel de Champlain 1604–1618,* p. 62.

32. Quoted in Russell, *Indian New England Before the Mayflower,* p. 174.

33. Weslager, *The Delaware Indians,* p. 39.

34. Hitakonanu'laxk, *The Grandfathers Speak,* p. 10.

35. John Heckewelder, *Thirty Thousand Miles with John Heckewelder,* ed. Paul A. W. Wallace. Pittsburgh: University of Pittsburgh Press, 1958, p. 116.

36. Champlain, *Voyages of Samuel de Champlain 1604–1618,* p. 55.

**Chapter 4: Spirits and Healing Powers**

37. Russell, *Indian New England Before the Mayflower,* p. 44.

38. Quoted in Simmons, *Spirit of the New England Tribes,* p. 39.

39. Quoted in Simmons, *Spirit of the New England Tribes,* p. 39.

40. Quoted in Simmons, *Spirit of the New England Tribes,* p. 40.

41. DeForest, *History of the Indians of Connecticut,* pp. 24–25.

42. Hitakonanu'laxk, *The Grandfathers Speak,* p. 32.

43. Hitakonanu'laxk, *The Grandfathers Speak,* p. 39.

44. Roger Williams, *The Complete Writings of Roger Williams,* vol. 1. New York: Russell & Russell, 1963, p. 152.

45. Quoted in Simmons, *Spirit of the New England Tribes,* p. 49.

46. William Bradford, *Bradford's History of Plymouth Plantation, 1606–1646.* 1856. Reprint, New York: Charles Scribner's Sons, 1908, p. 114.

47. Quoted in Simmons, *Spirit of the New England Tribes,* p. 53.

48. Quoted in Simmons, *Spirit of the New England Tribes,* p. 54.

49. Quoted in Sylvester, *Indian Wars of New England,* p. 31.

50. Quoted in Simmons, *Spirit of the New England Tribes,* p. 56.

51. Quoted in Simmons, *Spirit of the New England Tribes,* p. 57.

52. Heckewelder, *Thirty Thousand Miles with John Heckewelder,* p. 121.

53. Hitakonanu'laxk, *The Grandfathers Speak,* pp. 16–17.

54. Hitakonanu'laxk, *The Grandfathers Speak,* pp. 17–18.

**Chapter 5: War and Conflict in the Northeast**

55. DeForest, *History of the Indians of Connecticut,* p. 34.

56. DeForest, *History of the Indians of Connecticut,* p. 37.

57. Bradford, *Bradford's History of Plymouth Plantation, 1606–1646,* p. 110.

58. Horowitz, *The First Frontier,* p. 39.

59. John Mason, *A Brief History of the Pequot War.* 1656. Reprint, Ann Arbor, MI: University Microfilms, 1966, pp. 6–7.

60. Mason, *A Brief History of the Pequot War,* pp. 8–9.

61. Quoted in Horowitz, *The First Frontier,* p. 50.

62. Quoted in Horowitz, *The First Frontier,* p. 51.

63. Josephy, *500 Nations,* pp. 213–14.

64. William Hubbard, *The History of the Indian Wars in New England.* 1677. Reprint, New York: Kraus Reprint, 1969, pp. 180–81.

65. Quoted in Josephy, *500 Nations,* p. 216.

66. Quoted in Josephy, *500 Nations,* p. 217.

67. Colin G. Calloway, ed., *After King Philip's War.* Hanover, NH: University Press of New England, 1997, p. 2.

**Chapter 6: From King Philip to the Twenty-First Century**

68. William Apess, *On Our Own Ground.* Amherst, MA: University of Amherst Press, 1992, p. 240.

69. Calloway, *After King Philip's War,* p. 5.

70. Calloway, *After King Philip's War,* p. 6.

71. Calloway, *After King Philip's War,* p. 8.

72. Mashantucket Pequot Museum and Research Center, "Mashantucket Tribal Nation History," July 3, 1999. www.mashantucket.com/index1.html.

73. Simmons, *Spirit of the New England Tribes,* p. 207.

# For Further Reading

### Books

Peter Anastas, *Glooskap's Children*. Boston: Beacon Press, 1973. A book about the people of the Penobscot Nation who consider themselves the "original owners of Maine." The title character Glooskap is the legendary giant who created the Penobscot and who figures large in dozens of Penobscot legends that are included in the book.

Colin G. Calloway, *The Abenaki*. New York: Chelsea House Publishers, 1989. A richly detailed book about the Abenaki tribes in northern New England and Canada, their early modes of life, and their lives in modern times.

Hitakonanu'laxk, *The Grandfathers Speak*. New York: Interlink Books, 1994. The author, whose name translates as Tree Beard, is a chief of the Lenape tribe (also known as Delaware) who has done extensive research among his people to recover and retell tales and legends of how (among other things) people of his tribe were created on the back of a great turtle, how they were given the gift of fire, and how the Lenape people came to live along the Atlantic coast.

Alvin M. Josephy Jr., *500 Nations*. New York: Alfred A. Knopf, 1994. This superbly written book by a celebrated historian details the entire history of Native Americans from the earliest years when mastodons roamed the earth to the last battles and life on the reservations. Lavishly illustrated with paintings, woodcuts, drawings, and photos, many illustrating Native American artifacts, this book gives a detailed overview of America's five hundred Indian nations.

William S. Simmons, *The Narragansett*. New York: Chelsea House Publishers, 1989. A young-adult book that explores in detail the lives of the Narragansett tribe that once controlled most of what is now Rhode Island.

————, *Spirit of the New England Tribes.* Hanover, NH: University Press of New England, 1986. A book that represents one of the oldest continually recorded bodies of Native American folklore known in North America. Using over 240 original texts spanning three centuries, the book collects Native American legends, folktales, and traditional stories.

Laurie Weinstein-Farson, *The Wampanoag.* New York: Chelsea House Publishers, 1989. A young-adult book with detailed information about the Wampanoags of Massachusetts, written by an anthropology instructor at the University of Rhode Island and Mohegan Community College.

C. Keith Wilbur, *The New England Indians.* Chester, CT: The Globe Pequot Press, 1978. This book reconstructs the lives of the Native Americans who once inhabited New England. Hundreds of detailed line drawings illustrate step-by-step how natives built shelters, carved dugout canoes, grew food, hunted, fished, made tools and weapons, traveled, and more.

# Works Consulted

**Books**

William Apess, *On Our Own Ground.* Amherst, MA: University of Amherst Press, 1992. This book compiles the complete writings of William Apess, a Pequot who fought in the War of 1812, became a Methodist minister, and later fought for the rights of the Mashpee tribe on Cape Cod in the 1830s. The book contains *A Son of the Forest,* which was the first extended autobiography ever published by a Native American and which contains a full history of the native peoples of New England.

William Bradford, *Bradford's History of Plymouth Plantation, 1606–1646.* 1856. Reprint, New York: Charles Scribner's Sons, 1908. This work, written in 1669 and first printed in full in 1856, is a minor classic, reflecting the values of the small group of English separatists who became known as Pilgrims. The author was governor of Plymouth Colony for more than thirty years.

Colin G. Calloway, ed., *After King Philip's War.* Hanover, NH: University Press of New England, 1997. Edited by a professor of history and Native American studies at Dartmouth College, this book sheds light on the several hundred members of the Massachusetts tribes who survived King Philip's War and its immediate aftermath. The book traces their contribution as whalers, their contributions to fighting America's wars, and their lives into the late twentieth century.

Samuel de Champlain, *Voyages of Samuel de Champlain 1604–1618.* 1907. Reprint, New York: Barnes & Noble, 1946. A book taken from Champlain's diary as he explored Iroquois country in the 1600s before it had been changed by the Europeans. An important work of history that helps the reader understand the clash of cultures between the Europeans and the Indians.

Benjamin Church, *Diary of King Philip's War 1675–1676.* Chester, CT: Pequot Press, 1975. A detailed eyewitness account of King Philip's War as written by an English army captain who engineered the defeat of King Philip and the other New England tribes. A dry account of Native American life in seventeenth-century New England.

James Fenimore Cooper, *The Last of the Mohicans.* New York: Heritage Press, 1932. Cooper (1789–1851) was one of the first widely popular American novelists. *The Last of the Mohicans,* written in 1826, is an adventure set in the forest during the so-called French and Indian War, characterized by a series of thrilling attacks, escapes, and captures. Cooper's sympathy toward Native Americans is evident.

W. P. Cumming, S. E. Hillier, D. B. Quinn, G. Williams, *The Exploration of North America 1630–1776.* New York: G. P. Putnam's Sons, 1974. An in-depth book with many historical drawings and maps that covers the European exploration of North America, from New England to Florida to California and up to Alaska. Each chapter in the book is prefaced by historical events and routes taken, then gives eyewitness accounts from the explorers themselves.

John W. DeForest, *History of the Indians of Connecticut.* 1851. Reprint, New Haven, CT: Archon Books, 1964. First published in 1851, this book is one of the first and most detailed assessments of Native American life in Connecticut since the Pilgrim era. Although much of the text reveals the author's rampant prejudice against his subject, the writings are detailed and informative.

William A. Haviland and Marjory W. Power, *The Original Vermonters.* Hanover, NH: University Press of New England, 1981. The authors explore the lives of the Native Americans in Vermont before and after the arrival of the Europeans, mainly from an anthropological viewpoint.

John Heckewelder, *Thirty Thousand Miles with John Heckewelder.* Ed. Paul A. W. Wallace. Pittsburgh: University of Pittsburgh Press, 1958. Heckewelder was one of the most active and observant American travelers in the eighteenth century and spent the years from 1754 to 1813 writing about his adventures as a missionary in the service of the Moravian Church. His observations of the Native Americans are more sympathetic—and probably more accurate—than many writers of the time.

David Horowitz, *The First Frontier: The Indian Wars & America's Origins: 1607–1776.* New York: Simon & Schuster, 1978. This book is an honest look at American history that emphasizes that the American frontier belonged to six hundred Native American tribes before it was settled by Europeans. The book details the effect the French and English settlers and soldiers had on tribes from the Pilgrims to the American Revolution.

William Hubbard, *The History of the Indian Wars in New England.* 1677. Reprint, New York: Kraus Reprint, 1969. First printed in 1677, this book gives the one-sided English version of the Pequot War and King Philip's War. Native Americans are constantly referred to as "devils," "children of Satan," and other terms typical of the time.

Francis Jennings, *The Invasion of America.* Chapel Hill: University of North Carolina Press, 1975. Published by the Institute of Early American History and Culture, this book examines the "European invasion of America" from a Native American's viewpoint. The book also explores the sociocultural reasoning behind the Europeans' lack of regard for Native American land rights and beliefs.

John Mason, *A Brief History of the Pequot War.* 1656. Reprint, Ann Arbor, MI: University Microfilms, 1966. The history of the war made by the English against the Pequot tribe in Connecticut, first published in 1656, nineteen years after the events portrayed. The author was a major in the army that led the murderous charge against the Pequot.

Howard S. Russell, *Indian New England Before the Mayflower.* Hanover, NH: University Press of New England, 1980. This book is an interesting study of New England Native American life before it was disrupted by European settlers. The author covers subjects concerning everyday life of the natives, with many details about food, agriculture, and hunting.

Herbert Milton Sylvester, *Indian Wars of New England.* Vol. 1. Boston: W. B. Clarke Company, 1910. Volume 1 of three massive books of seven hundred pages each, detailing the dozens of wars fought in New England in which Native Americans participated—including the Pequot War, King Philip's War, and others. The author treats his subjects with great disrespect and prejudice, but covers the history very thoroughly.

Clinton Alfred Weslager, *The Delaware Indians.* New Brunswick, NJ: Rutgers University Press, 1972. An informative book that traces the history of the Delaware tribe from its ancient homeland on the East Coast along the Delaware River to their modern-day home on an Oklahoma reservation.

Roger Williams, *The Complete Writings of Roger Williams.* Vol. 1. New York: Russell & Russell, 1963. Roger Williams (1603–1683) was a radical Puritan thinker and founder of the colony of Rhode Island. He insisted that the lands given to the Puritans still belonged to the Native Americans. Williams worked among the natives and earned their friendship, which enabled him to learn their language and to write *A Key into the Language of America,* which is part of this seven-volume work.

**Websites**

**Geographic Overview of First Nations Histories** (www.dickshovel. com/up.html). When completed, the site will encompass approximately 240 tribal histories grouped by geographic region. The tribes of the Northeast are fully covered, with pages of information about each one.

**Indians of Pennsylvania and the Delaware Valley** (www. communicator. com/indianpa.html). Good links to tribal websites.

**The Mashantucket Pequot Museum and Research Center** (www.mashantucket.com/index1.html). This homepage details the history of the Pequot in Connecticut.

**The Mohegan Tribe Home Page** (www.mohegan.nsn.us/ tribe/home.html). The website of the Mohegan tribes that details the history and customs of the Mohegans in Connecticut.

**The Narragansett Indian Home Page** (www.chariho.k12.ri.us/ cyber fair98/chanarra.htm). Has history and links to other tribal websites.

**The Powhatan Ranape Home Page** (www.powhatan.org/). The Powhatan Renape Nation is located at the Rankokus Indian Reservation in Westampton Township, Burlington County, New Jersey.

**The Ramapough Nation** (www.ramapoughnation.org/). The Ramapough Mountain Indians are a tribe of about three thousand Native Americans living on the New York/New Jersey border.

# Index

# Picture Credits

Cover photo: Corbis
Archive Photos, 33, 70, 79
Corbis, 38
Corbis-Bettmann, 54, 89
Corbis/Dave G. Houser, 12
Corbis/Hulton-Deutsch Collection, 45
Houghton Library, Harvard University, 15
Illinois State Historical Library, 67
Library of Congress, 20, 28, 36, 58, 63, 77, 82, 85
Mashantucket Pequot Museum and Research Center, 91
North Wind Picture Archives, 9, 21, 24, 30, 32, 37, 42, 44, 50, 51,
    61, 72, 74, 84, 87
Prints Old & Rare, 11

# About the Author

Stuart A. Kallen is the author of more than 145 nonfiction books for children and young adults. He has written on topics ranging from the theory of relativity to rock-and-roll history to life on the American frontier. In addition, Mr. Kallen has written award-winning children's videos and television scripts. In his spare time, Stuart A. Kallen is a singer/songwriter/guitarist in San Diego, California.